FROM RACE TO RENEWAL

It's Not All Black & White

ARNIE SIDMAN

ISBN: 1497306388
ISBN 13: 9781497306387

"Though this nation has proudly thought of itself as an ethnic melting pot, in things racial we have always been and continue to be, in too many ways, essentially a nation of cowards. . . . [W]e, average Americans, simply do not talk enough with each other about race."

U.S. Attorney General Eric Holder
February 18, 2009

"A white American man would have to be a fool to talk about race in America today. Fortunately, I qualify."

Arnie Sidman
January 16, 2014

PROLOGUE

Over the years, I have become concerned about what I perceive to be an inexorable drift in American society—a malaise that threatens our heritage, our precious legacy. My 20-year career in corporate America afforded me a special opportunity to observe not only my beloved country but also many other parts of the putative civilized world. Without a doubt, Team America is *numero uno*—but only because we're up against such weak competition.

Even a casual observer such as I could easily conclude in the 1970s that the Europeans would never get their act together. It was almost impossible to find an EU flag outside of Brussels. Oh, they had some fine players—spectacular food and architecture, too—but they were frequently at each other. A cursory review of their history—pick any century—confirmed for me that they had no idea how to play the game of life.

And what about us, our team? We wouldn't even exist in anything like our present form if the Europeans—aided and abetted by other "teams"—hadn't treated our ancestors so badly. Whether by the grace of God or historical accident, we Americans have been granted an unparalleled opportunity to show the world how to play the game of life—and we are blowing it.

For myself, I have always believed that life was a team game where individual achievement was necessary but not sufficient. It's just no fun being a good—even a great—player on a bad team. Every player on the team must be given an opportunity to play, and every player on the team must contribute something to team success and be compensated accordingly. If a player gets injured, the team should "carry" the player for a while, but no player should expect to be carried indefinitely.

Our country was founded by people who valued freedom over security. Over time, it seems to me, we have become a nation that values security over freedom. And in recent years, we have expanded the concept of security to include just about anything we don't want to be bothered about. We have lost our sense of responsibility and accountability and have become increasingly self-absorbed. As the ditty goes, we're beginning to look a lot like Eur-ope.

My own most significant contribution to our slide has to do with race. I remember precisely when I became aware of the fact that I was uncomfortable around blacks *en masse* in personal settings. I remember precisely the day I walked down Constitution Avenue to catch my bus to avoid the crowd listening to the Rev. Dr. Martin Luther King, Jr. deliver his "Dream" speech—not my problem. I remember precisely the circumstances under which I discovered that I would never ever consider moving into a black neighborhood.

The circumstances under which I entered corporate America forced me to confront my malady head on. Fortunately, although I was embarrassed to admit to myself that I had this problem, I would have been even more ashamed not to try to remedy it. So, over time, I just started "showing up" in the black community. Bless you, Woody Allen. And, glory be to God, over time, my condition improved. Oh, don't get me wrong—I wasn't cured; more like an AA alumnus. But much of my discomfort disappeared.

The downside for me occurred when I came to the realization that there was a real limit to how much I could improve without some help. To that end, I tried to enlist both black and white community leaders to help me out for what I perceived to be the good of our team. The rationalizations I heard for continuing to ignore the issue underscored just how naïve I was about the impenetrability of the race taboo.

I believe our inability to confront our racial hang-ups has been a significant contributing factor leading to the moral drift noted earlier.

We really need to address this congenital defect in our body politic. That is why I wrote this book.

ONE

My wife, Toby, and I moved to Atlanta in September 1987. I was part of a small cadre of RJR Nabisco corporate staff officers moving there from Winston-Salem, North Carolina. The sheer size of the company and exaggerated notoriety of its chief executive officer, F. Ross Johnson, made this otherwise unremarkable corporate headquarters relocation a minor media event. From a business and community development standpoint, however, local Atlantans had every reason to believe that financial opportunity was knocking, and real estate brokers, financial institutions and other service providers rolled out the red carpet. Local non-profits did likewise, as visions of corporate contributions danced in their heads. Although the local citizenry would soon enough discover that the reality resembled the Land of Oz, I decided to try to take full advantage of the corporate perquisites and visibility afforded by the move. Accordingly, over the next few months, Toby and I accepted a number of invitations that we felt would help smooth our entry into our new home.

This extraordinary transition notwithstanding, there was one aspect of our new environment that had not been made available to us by invitation, so we sought it out. We attended a formal testimonial dinner held at a large hotel in downtown Atlanta on the evening of March 17, 1988. We did not expect to know anyone in attendance at that event; and, in fact, we did not recognize one familiar face that entire evening. The dinner honored the retiring Atlanta Public Schools Superintendent Alonzo A. Crim, and served as a fund-raiser to help Crim establish a chair at Georgia State University in honor of the late Benjamin E. Mays, former president of the Atlanta Board of Education and Morehouse College.

Neither of our children was eligible to attend Atlanta's public schools. Eric, our eldest, was in college. Steven, our youngest, was living with good friends of ours in Winston-Salem so that he could complete his senior year in high school there. On the surface, there was no apparent reason for us to be in attendance at that dinner.

Ah, but there was a reason. Simply put, by that stage of my life, I had made up my mind to try to improve race relations between blacks and whites in America; that Atlanta was the best place to start trying; and that Ross Johnson, RJR Nabisco's CEO, was God's instrument for getting me there. On the evening of March 17, 1988, I was on a reconnaissance mission. The only reason Toby and I were in attendance at that dinner on that evening was that we expected most of the attendees to be black. Most were.

TWO

I don't recall having any real contact with blacks while I was growing up in Washington, D.C., on the west side of Rock Creek Park, the white side of town. Lafayette Elementary, Alice Deal Junior High, and Woodrow Wilson High had children in attendance from all over the globe, but I don't remember any black American children in attendance at any of those institutions during the years immediately following World War II. My grandmother had a deaf black maid named Mabel. I tried to speak to her from time to time, but it was difficult for us to communicate. My greatest concern as a seven-year-old was that I not frighten her when I approached her from the rear.

One summer, our Walter Johnson League twelve-and-under baseball team advanced to the playoffs, and the word was that we might have to play a black baseball team. The word also was that these kids were good, a lot better than us, and that we were gonna get our butts kicked. I think we did get our butts kicked; I know we lost, at least in part because we were uncomfortable playing downtown.

My only other recollection of early encounters with blacks also involved baseball. I loved watching the Washington Senators try to play major league baseball. Sometimes my grandfather took me. He had been a pretty good semi-pro player in his day, and he regaled me with baseball lore and strategy. Most of the time, though, it was a friend and I who took the M 4 Tenley Circle bus to 30th Street; transferred to the M 2 for the ride on Military Road east to the other side of Rock Creek Park; and transferred once again for the Georgia Avenue streetcar ride south to 7th and Florida Avenue and good old Griffith Stadium. For a buck and a quarter, you could see batting and fielding practice and a double header. If you got there at 11:00 a.m., when the park opened, that money could get you eight hours of baseball-induced joy (though slightly muted by frustration at the Senators' lack of skill). You could also get a good general admission seat in the upper deck behind first base with an unobstructed view of most of the field.

But what I remember most was the crowd that occupied those upper deck seats. There were lots of black men, mostly elderly, with leathery and wrinkled skin, gold fillings and lots of smiles. With them, I spent the whole day talking about the weather, the field conditions, the standings, the scores, the pitch-by-pitch strategy, and the defensive alignment. Together we second-guessed every-body in sight—the managers, the players, the umpires, the vendors ("No way he should've thrown that hot dog!"), and the crowd in the bleachers. In spite of our opinions, we were men of few words: "Did you see that?", "Just stood there with the bat on his shoulders", "Threw him a change-up on a 3-1 count" (accompanied by a head shake and a roll of the eyes). We laughed 'til tears came to our eyes, joshed each other, called each other names, and had a grand old time. I loved being there with those men. I never asked nor learned one of their names. Except for two or three of them, I don't remem-ber seeing the same face twice.

It was a little different when I went to the ball games with my grandfather. We hardly talked to the black men seated near us. My grandfather was a cab driver, primarily operating in downtown Washington. He felt that black cab drivers were given prefer-ence by black bellmen at the downtown hotels. He referred to all black people as *shvartzehs*, a Yiddish derivation from the German word for "black." Sometimes when he used the term, that was all it meant: "black." On other occasions, though it was intended to be disparaging or disrespectful. Most of the time I could tell the difference because of the context, or based on his tone of voice or body language.

There was more going on around me than I had yet grasped, and one thing in particular that I came to understand sometime later. The Cleveland Indians always drew big crowds and lots of applause from the men of the upper deck. I didn't know it then, but in 1947, the Indians had broken the American League color line with Larry Doby and Luke Easter. I don't remember how old I was when the realization hit me that, for many of the men sitting in the seats around me, cheering for the black players and the team that recruited the black players was more important than what happened to the Washington Senators.

More to the point, while growing up in Washington, D.C., immediately after World War II, what blacks were called, or what they were doing, or anything else about their lives, had nothing to do with my life. To the extent that I acknowledged their existence, they were colored people. I didn't need to acknowledge their existence very often.

All of that changed for me in 1955 when, at age 14, I made the decision to attend summer school. In those days, eligible students in the D.C. public school system graduated either in the winter or in June, with most students programmed for the latter. Winter graduation cohorts were social misfits in the annual school calendar and were ultimately phased out. For me, however, the only way out of the winter graduation class was either to drop back a half-year or to "skip" ahead a semester. In those days, Jewish boys didn't drop back. Jewish boys were expected to be excellent students. Staying back was seen as the antithesis of academic excellence, so I resigned myself to attending summer school, which was a pre-requisite to skipping.

My decision to attend summer school had not come easily. Everybody knew that summer schoolers were mostly goof-offs and hell-raisers—juvenile delinquents who smoked behind the teacher's back and didn't care how they performed in school. To make matters worse, I had heard that there were going to be black kids at

Roosevelt High School that summer, presumably in response to the Supreme Court's 1954 decision in *Brown v. Board of Education*.

Roosevelt was on the other side of town, so I arranged to ride with two of my Wilson High schoolmates. As far as I could tell, Bobby Goldstein, Al Marsh and I were the only white students at Roosevelt that summer, and I was the only white student in Mrs. T's English class.

Mrs. T began right after the opening bell: "Students, welcome to class. We have a lot to cover in a short time, so pay attention. I'm going to call the roll now. The office hasn't had time to alphabetize the roll so listen closely and raise your hand when I call your name. Class participation is an important part of your grade. In a couple of days, I will know each of you by name."

I was trying to get my bearings as Mrs. T started to call the roll. Attention gave way to discomfort with the unknown—what was I going to do as a white kid in class with a whole crowd of black kids?

The roll call continued. I was paying no attention until it dawned on me that Mrs. T was calling a name that sounded vaguely familiar.

"Mr. Sidney Arnold," she called. No student raised his hand. Again: "Mr. Sidney Arnold." Stillness; quiet; no response. "Mr. Arnold, are you here?" Haltingly, I raised my hand. "Thank you Mr. Arnold."

Day one was a total fog—I was inexplicably uncomfortable. But on day two, I distinctly remember that Mrs. T established who was in control of her class.

J.D. was a fairly tall, good-looking young man with an irrepressible grin and a personality to match.

Mrs. T was writing something on the blackboard with her back to the class. J.D. threw something across the room that landed audibly.

"Mr. D," said Mrs. T softly, but firmly, "did you launch a projectile across the room?" Mrs. T was still facing the blackboard.

"No, ma'am," J.D. responded crisply.

Mrs. T turned to face the class. "Mr. D, I repeat. Did you launch a projectile across the room?"

"No, ma'am," J.D. responded.

"Mr. D, you certainly are well trained."

"Yes, ma'am," Mr. J.D. agreed.

"Mr. Well-trained D, that's who you are. Mr. Well-trained D," concluded Mrs. T.

And it was "Well-trained" or "Mr. D" for the rest of the semester.

Mrs. T spoke perfect English with no discernible dialect. This was a total surprise to me. In my mind's eye I had pictured blacks as a little slow of speech, with an exaggerated southern drawl peppered with malapropisms.

This view of black speech was based in large part on my observations at Griffith Stadium, as confirmed by *The Amos 'n' Andy Show*.

Amos 'n' Andy was an early television sitcom—the first network show with an all-black cast—that depicted black life from the vantage point of the "Mystic Knights of the Sea" lodge brothers, a Harlem-based organization. The show ran on CBS from 1951 to 1953, and I loved it. Many of the characters were admirable: Sapphire and Sapphire's Momma, for example. Some were hilarious—the conniving Kingfish; Calhoun, the slippery lawyer; and Andrew H. Brown, a.k.a. Andy, the master of the malapropism: "Pardon me for protrudin'," he would intone, prior to interrupting a private conversation among others.

In retrospect, airing when it did during the 1950s, *The Amos 'n' Andy Show* probably reinforced the image of blacks in America. It wasn't until much later that I learned that CBS had withdrawn the show in 1966, at least in part because of protests made by the NAACP.[1] At the time I never thought anything about it. But, then again, in the 1950s, I didn't think much about blacks or their concerns at all.

Mrs. T defied all the expectations that Andy and the men of the upper deck at Griffith Stadium had given me. She hammered home the importance of correct speech and implored us to care about the rules of written and spoken English.

It seemed that Mrs. T had developed a story for every rule: "If you're sitting at home one afternoon listening to your records, and you hear a knock at the door, and you say 'who's there?' and the person outside calls back, 'It's me. Open the door.' Don't you open that door. Don't you dare open that door until the person outside says, 'It is I. It is I. It is I.'"

By the end of the first week of summer school I had not uttered one word in class. About the middle of the second week, my fear of a poor grade in oral recitation overtook my fear of calling attention to myself. I raised my hand in response to a question posed by Mrs. T. "Well, Mr. Arnold, I was wondering when you were going to join the class."

Mrs. T was special. As I think about her now, I see an amalgamation of Ethel Waters and Maya Angelou. Tough, yet soft. Intelligent, yet patient. Distant, yet caring. Her remarkable presence drew me out of my discomfort and into the game. Soon, "Sidney" or "Mr. Arnold" was a regular participant in class.

Before I realized it, the summer session was over. Mrs. T stood before us for the last time: "The roll has now been alphabetized," said Mrs. T, eloquently as ever. "Raise your hand as I call your name. I will be recording your oral recitation grade as your name is called."

Somewhere in the middle of the list, she hesitated, and looked quizzically at the sheet before her:

"Mr. Arnold Sidman," she said. "Mr. Arnold Sidman."

Stillness; quiet; no response. Again: "Mr. Arnold Sidman".

Mrs. T was just about to move on to the next name when I raised my hand. I stared straight ahead, trying not to make eye contact with Mrs. T. My feeling of embarrassment was overwhelming.

I did not say more than a total of 50 words to my classmates that summer. No one approached me in conversation. And I never got comfortable enough or concerned enough to approach anyone seeking conversation. I just wanted to get my credits and be done with it.

I am still at a loss to explain what I experienced as a student in Mrs. T's class at Roosevelt High School in the summer of 1955. Somehow, I was overwhelmed with the contemplation of blacks as a group in a social context. I call this particular discomfort with blacks *en masse* the Sidney Syndrome.

Although I have matured somewhat since discovering I was afflicted with the Sidney Syndrome, I am unhappy to report that I am still somewhat uncomfortable in an intimate social context with black people unknown to me. My experience tells me that most white Americans are similarly afflicted. If I am correct, then my problem, multiplied by tens of millions over the centuries, has created a huge problem for black Americans, which in turn is problematic for America.

THREE

Ibelieve that God exists; that God is purposeful; that God is concerned with man; and that God has endowed man with free will.
I need to believe this because if man is merely going through the
motions, then my life is meaningless.

My tradition informs me that God spoke to a man named Moses,
who, although raised as a member of the Egyptian aristocracy,
identified with the Hebrew slaves.

God came to Moses, telling him that he had seen the affliction
of his people in Egypt, and that he would set them free and take
them to a new land. Moses expressed his doubts about his ability to
implement God's plan, that he was "slow of speech" and thus would
be unable to convince either the Egyptian pharaoh or the Hebrew
slaves.

My tradition also informs me that a man named George
Washington also believed in the Divine Providence. Although
raised an aristocrat with a formal allegiance to the King of England,
he identified with the natural rights of Virginians and, ultimately,
of all American colonists.

Like Moses, Washington was "called" to duty in the service of
his people. Washington, like Moses, was not a gifted public speaker,
and expressed doubts as to his ability to accomplish what was asked
of him. But the people believed in Washington, as they had believed
in Moses.[2]

During negotiations with the British, King George III hardened his
position, thus creating pressure on the American people to overcome
the psychological barrier to declaring independence. Washington,
like Moses, understood that his role was to remove this barrier while
preventing his people from being annihilated.

During the Revolutionary War, the American colonists saw themselves as the new Children of Israel, whose leader, George Washington, was going to take them to the Promised Land according to the Divine Plan. Divine Providence was said to accompany the colonists, who nevertheless complained to Washington of the hardships attendant upon independence, just as the Hebrews had complained to Moses. And later, after the death of Washington, it was said that it was our "manifest destiny to overspread and to possess the whole of the continent which Providence has given us for the development of the great experiment of liberty and federative self government entrusted to us."[3]

We Americans are the beneficiaries of a precious legacy, a great estate: unsurpassed individual freedom; limited government of, by, and for the people; and a history of the peaceful, voluntary transfer of power delegated by the people pursuant to the lawful exercise of the right to vote. Our Declaration of Independence, Constitution, and Bill of Rights are not dead letters—they continue to guide us in our daily lives. We cherish our ideals, and the rights of all our citizens, even when we forget those ideals and transgress those rights. We accept the yoke of individual responsibility, even as we seek daily to extricate ourselves from it. And we enjoy the material blessings that peace, freedom and self-sufficiency make possible.

No great estate is debt-free, no great inheritance unencumbered. God's promise to Israel was always conditional; it was a continuing covenantal relationship. *If* Israel would obey Torah principles, *then* God would support Israel. *If* Israel would pursue justice and righteousness, *then* the blessings would follow. What are those obligations that accompany *our* inheritance? And to whom are they owed?

FOUR

In 1957, President Eisenhower sent U.S. Army troops to enforce the integration order at Central High School in Little Rock, Arkansas. I was aware of the turmoil occurring in the South concerning integration of the schools, but I was not surprised about it. I understood that southerners were prejudiced against blacks. As far as I was concerned, the South was a foreign country you had to drive through to get from Washington, D.C., to Miami Beach.

President Eisenhower was pretty clear about his reason for sending in the troops. He wasn't sure he agreed with the Supreme Court's holding that the U.S. Constitution required that public schools be integrated. He was sure that he had pledged to defend and protect the Constitution of the United States, and he was not going to back down on his pledge. He was committed to enforcing validly issued U.S. judicial decrees. It was that simple.

❋ ❋ ❋

By the spring of 1961, I had been accepted to Georgetown University Law Center in Washington, D.C. I knew I wanted to practice law. I also knew I wanted to marry Toby Tarlow, whom I had met when she was a freshman at Russell Sage College and I was a junior at Rensselaer Polytechnic Institute.

By 1963, my life was beginning to take on some direction. I was intrigued by tax law—its arcane rules, its breadth, and the idea that the adversary was the government. One of my conjured concerns regarding the practice of law was "shysters"—lawyers who would do anything to win regardless of ethical considerations. I knew I would be constrained by ethical standards, and I did not want to be competing against other lawyers who did not feel themselves similarly constrained. I was fairly certain government lawyers would feel themselves constrained by ethical standards.

I had come to these judgments about ethical standards and government lawyers by observing my father and his colleagues, almost all of whom had joined the government during the Depression.

To me, the lawyers among them represented the legal profession at its best. Almost without exception, they, like Dad, were intelligent, concerned citizens. Although they often disagreed, the issue (as described by Dad at the dinner table, with confidential facts carefully excised) was nearly always about what was right, just or fair. They took their responsibilities seriously (themselves somewhat less so). Integrity was their watchword. I knew I wanted to live with that kind of probity; I felt confident tax law was the right profession for me.

●　●　●

Toby had transferred to George Washington University in 1961 when I began law school. She graduated from G.W. on June 5, 1963. Immediately thereafter, we drove from Washington to her home in Massachusetts, where we were married at a synagogue in Salem on June 9. We drove to Quebec City for our honeymoon and back to Washington so we could begin work at our summer jobs on Monday, June 17. Toby had found a retail sales position at Garfinkel's, and I had landed a summer intern position with the IRS Chief Counsel's office.

Blacks were still not on my radar screen. Denial of civil rights was a southern problem, not my problem. I was in favor of civil rights for blacks. As a resident of the District of Columbia, I had been denied the vote for either members of Congress or the president until 1960. I knew what denial of voting rights meant to me. Still, the pieces weren't coming together just yet—I confronted the problems facing black Americans only when they stood directly in my path.

On August 28, 1963, a huge civil rights march was scheduled to take place in downtown Washington just across the street from my office. Our office was being closed early to allow us to leave the area without personal penalty. The expectation was there might be trouble in connection with the march.

I left the office in the early afternoon. My curiosity about the marchers was sufficiently piqued to cause me to walk down Constitution Avenue toward the crowd. I wasn't interested in listening to speeches. I surveyed the gathering for about ten minutes; the crowd was huge, the air was quiet, and the spirit of the people almost reverential. Many in the crowd were white, which somewhat surprised me.

I walked back down Constitution Avenue and never gave another thought to what I had witnessed. The next day, I learned that the crowd might have exceeded 200,000. I'm not sure when I learned that the Rev. Dr. Martin Luther King, Jr. had delivered his "Dream" speech at that march.

In September, I returned for my last year of undergraduate law. Toby commenced her career as a second-grade teacher at the Margaret Brent Elementary School in Prince Georges County, Maryland. The school was located in the general vicinity of NASA's Goddard Space Flight Center, and many of the school's parent body were employed there. The intellectual capacity of many of these students reflected the advanced degrees held by their parents, and Toby kiddingly observed that she was holding her own with most of them.

On November 22, 1963, Toby called me from a pay phone at her school. The teachers had just been informed that President Kennedy had been shot in Dallas. She asked me to turn on the radio to find out what was happening.

It wasn't long before the entire country heard the news. President Kennedy, our first Roman Catholic president, had been assassinated.

President Kennedy had been elected following a campaign in which his religion had been an issue. Neither Toby nor I was surprised about that. Growing up, we had each become aware of neighborhoods where Jews couldn't live and country clubs that Jews couldn't join. We were also vaguely aware of job discrimination directed against Jews, but had not had any such personal experiences. Toby and I were pleased when President Kennedy was elected. We hoped it indicated increasing tolerance for religious minorities in America.

Unfortunately, my interest in religious and ethnic tolerance did not extend to matters of race. During my tenure as an IRS employee, the only black person I remember was a secretary who was very attractive from the neck up but obese from the neck down. She walked only with difficulty. She was visited from time to time by other blacks. I was told she was involved with government labor union organizing. What I remember most was the sign she displayed prominently on her desk: "Do a little more work each day, and each day a little more work will be expected of you."

FIVE

I t was a typical late summer in Washington in 1968—hot and humid. My four-year commitment to the IRS Chief Counsel's office, which I had signed following graduation from law school, was completed. I had been interviewing almost exclusively with law firms in or around Washington since April with a notable lack of success. I had been an editor of the *Georgetown Law Journal* and had obtained an LL.M. degree in taxation at Georgetown at night. I was seeking an associate position in tax. It wasn't happening.

I received a telephone call from a gentleman who represented himself to be employed by the R. J. Reynolds Tobacco Co. He indicated the company was seeking to hire a tax lawyer with federal and international tax background. "We would like to interview you," he said.

For at least ten years, I had envisioned myself as a lawyer practicing in Washington. Anyone who knew me well had the same expectation. I had no concept of what a lawyer would do in a corporate context. I had no idea where R. J. Reynolds was located or how they had gotten my name. I declined the invitation.

About a month later the gentleman called back. "We're back in town for the day conducting interviews. We sure would like to talk to you."

"I'm sorry; I'm really busy today," I said.

"Well, how about after work?"

I met the gentlemen from R. J. Reynolds at the cocktail lounge in National Airport. In those days, Piedmont Airlines had direct flights from National to Smith Reynolds Airport in Winston-Salem where Reynolds' headquarters were located.

We chatted while they waited for their flight to board.

The basic proposition was simple. In 1964, the U.S. surgeon general had proclaimed smoking had negative health implications. In 1966, new federal legislation mandated that cigarette packages display health warnings. Tobacco companies anticipated some slowdown in the growth rates of their domestic cigarette businesses, and were diversifying through acquisitions and international expansion. Reynolds was staffing up for this effort.

An added bonus was also evident. I liked these people. They seemed to like me. I was intrigued. They offered to fly my wife and me to Winston-Salem for a couple of days.

"I'll need to call home and check with her," I responded.

After hanging up the pay phone, I returned to the gentlemen at the table. "I think we can work it out. I have just one request. We want to see if Winston-Salem has a Jewish community. We don't need a ghetto, but we need at least one viable synagogue."

"That can be arranged," the personnel man responded. "I know the rabbi."

●　●　●

Winston-Salem and the Piedmont region of North Carolina turned out to be a lot prettier than the areas I traversed as a child on the way to Florida via U.S. 301. Lush rolling hills abounded and a variety of trees dotted the landscape. At one thousand feet elevation above sea level, the late summer humidity seemed considerably less oppressive than that which chronically beset Washington in that season. We also learned that Winston-Salem was reputed to be one of the wealthiest cities in the country. R. J. Reynolds and his successors had been firm believers in employee profit sharing, and the entire community had benefited from the tobacco largesse. I was reminded of my work on the Treasury Department's report on private philanthropic foundations; I had been amazed that a disproportionately large number of these foundations were founded and maintained in North Carolina.

The best part of the encounter was the people. Everyone was warm, friendly and open about issues and opportunities. As each hour passed, Toby and I were beginning to envision ourselves in this strange new world and liking it.

David S. Peoples, the chief financial officer, was my last interviewer. He too was warm and friendly, with a knowing grin and a Tennessee drawl. After a short while he came right to the point: "Well, Arnold, it appears that you have made quite a favorable impression on our people. Is there anything you would like to ask me?"

I was impressed by the fact the chief financial officer was part of the interview process. It seemed possible the job was going to be as challenging, and the opportunity as great, as the picture they were painting. I wanted the job, but I did have some concerns.

"Yes, sir, there is. I'm Jewish, I'm a Yankee, and I don't smoke. Which one of these is going to hurt me the most?"

Dave Peoples reflected just momentarily, then grinned and responded: "Arnold, if you do start smoking, we sure hope you'll consider our brands."

By the time we left for home, Toby and I had already made our decision. If they made any reasonable offer, I was going to accept it. There was one viable synagogue with a rabbi. And the R. J. Reynolds Tobacco Co. wanted to employ me, warts and all.

I commenced my career with Reynolds in October 1968. Toby and I decided to rent a small townhouse near the city center. We figured if things didn't work out, it would be easier to extricate ourselves from a lease than to sell an owned home. The only negative attribute of the townhouse was its proximity to the area of town where "racial disorder" had occurred a year earlier.

In July of 1967, President Johnson established a National Advisory Commission on Civil Disorders in response to a series of riots that had occurred in cities across the country. The Commission produced a huge report that became popularly known as the Kerner

Report. (Otto Kerner, then Governor of Illinois, had chaired the Commission.) The Kerner Report noted the following:

- The civil disorders of 1967 involved Negroes acting against local symbols of white American society, authority and property in Negro neighborhoods—rather than against white persons.

- Of 164 disorders reported during the first nine months of 1967, eight (5 percent) were major in terms of violence and damage; 33 (20 percent) were serious but not major; 123 (75 percent) were minor and undoubtedly would not have received national attention as "riots" had the nation not been sensitized by the more serious outbreaks.

- In the 75 disorders studied by a Senate subcommittee, 83 deaths were reported. Eighty-two percent of the deaths, and more than half the injuries occurred in Newark and Detroit. About 10 percent of the dead and 38 percent of the injured were public employees, primarily law officers and firemen. The overwhelming majority of the persons killed or injured in all the disorders were Negro civilians.[4]

My impression of the Winston-Salem "riot," based entirely on hearsay, was that it was similar to the "minor" outbreaks described in the Commission Report. In any event I was much more concerned about my career and the issues I had raised with Dave Peoples: tobacco, Yankee and Jew.

Notably, the Yankee problem stemmed from my ignorance of southern history and culture. It was not uncommon for northerners to adopt an attitude of moral, and even intellectual, superiority in their relations with southerners. The stereotypical southerner was provincial, backward, narrow-minded, and an incipient bigot. Slavery, and subsequent subjugation of black Americans, were deemed to be activities practiced almost exclusively by southerners.

Growing up in Washington, D.C., I considered the Potomac River to be the dividing line between the North and the South. And even though our nation's capital had a very southern flavor in those days, I was proud to be on the side of the angels—the side that had won the Civil War. Nevertheless, there was ample evidence the Civil War was very much a continuing conflict in the minds of many southerners.

All of this was quickly forgotten within months of our move to Winston-Salem. The southerners I met and dealt with were highly intelligent. The tax department head who hired me turned out to be brilliant. He was the first individual I had ever met outside the bounds of academia who had earned an S. J. D. degree, the legal equivalent of a Ph.D. He was both a visionary strategist and a tactician. He was a rigorous analyst and a keen political observer. He was diligent in executing his assignments and expected the same from his subordinates. And finally, beneath a misleadingly gruff exterior beat the heart of a fine person. He was one among many I admired in the new southern culture we entered in Winston-Salem.

Initially, we also felt uneasy about assimilating into a new religious community, but not in the way you might suspect. Our conflict was never with those of other faiths; from the very beginning we had many Christian friends and neighbors. All in all, I was quite comfortable with Christians. As it turned out, the most problematic aspect of our move to Winston-Salem related to the nature of the Jewish community there. Both Toby and I had been raised in a liberal orthodox Jewish tradition. The only substantial Jewish house of worship in Winston-Salem was affiliated with the Union of American Hebrew Congregations, the Reform movement.

During my younger years, my father's principal involvement outside of work was participation at the *shul*, or synagogue. He had spent close to ten years trying to effect an amalgamation of three orthodox synagogues: Tifereth Israel (of which he was an officer),

Agudas Achim, and Ohev Shalom. The proposed alliance was to be known by the acronym TAOS. On many an evening he would return from a meeting in utter frustration, once adding that he felt the acronym should be changed to CHAOS. Added to the normal issues associated with institutional mergers were questions of ritual and halachic interpretation. My father had achieved a fine reputation at the IRS as a reasonable man, consensus builder, and mediator. All of this was unavailing in the cutthroat world of synagogue politics. Not surprisingly, TAOS never got off the ground. The three synagogues went their separate ways, two of them housed in new buildings directly opposite one another at 16th and Juniper streets. Knowing all of this, the concept of Jewish peoplehood didn't enter my consciousness during my formative years. On the contrary, my early notions of Jewish communal life were the antithesis of any unifying Jewish theme.

But the myth of Jewish unity was even more strikingly portrayed to me in my youth when it came to the issue of Reform Judaism.

As I was led to believe, Jews affiliated with the Reform movement were non-observant Jews who structured their service and constructed their houses of worship in a manner which it was hoped would be most acceptable to American Christians. Reform Jews were seen by my family as inauthentic apologists who were intent upon assimilation into American society even if that required abandonment of the tradition. American classical liberal Reform meant prayer in the English vernacular rather than Hebrew, and accompanied by an organ rather than *a cappella*. On *shabbos*, Reform Jews drove to Temple rather than walked to *shul*. Reform Jews did not wear a *yarmulke* or *tallith* during morning prayers. Reform Jews ate leavened bread during Passover and did not fast on Yom Kippur.

Of course, not all orthodox Jews obeyed all the rules all the time. My family drove to *shul* on *shabbos*, but we parked on the street near the synagogue, not on the parking lot adjacent thereto. We knew we were in violation of the rule prohibiting "work" on *shabbos*, but we compromised. In contrast, Reform Jews denied the existence of the rule altogether and this was unthinkable to families like ours. But, in 1968, if Toby and I were to move to Winston-Salem, and if we wished to become part of that Jewish community, for all practical purposes we would have to become Reform Jews.

SIX

I had been promoted to the position of corporate tax manager in 1970. I was feeling pretty good about our decision to move to Winston-Salem. The mild euphoria was short-lived. A few months following my elevation, a colleague approached me in a confidential manner:

"Arnie, I don't mind you being promoted, but I hope you don't intend to bring in any more."

Any more what? Non-smokers? Yankees? Jews? I assumed he meant the latter. I refused to dignify his remark with a response.

As a new manager in corporate headquarters, I was invited to attend a meeting regarding the company's commitment to affirmative action. The presentation was made by the personnel department manager responsible for monitoring our compliance with the federal program mandated for companies selling goods or services to the federal government. The presenter was a distinguished-looking black man, a retired military officer.

He explained the company's interpretation of the law as requiring a strong effort to hire more "females and minorities" in manager and professional positions. As a company, our hiring practices would be judged by whether our employee demographics gave adequate representation to the protected class of females and minorities.

In other words, we could be found guilty of discrimination regardless of our benign intent if our results indicated underutilization of women and minorities. My mind began to wander:

> *I am supportive of equal opportunity for all: no person should be denied a job on account of color, race, religion, gender or any other category. But affirmative action? For "minorities"? What kind of minorities? My father's parents were Eastern European*

immigrants with no English language skills when they arrived in America. They never learned to read English, although they learned to speak it. My grandfather earned a modest living as a paperhanger. He spoke with an accent. Where was his affirmative action? Of course he was white, but he was Jewish. Black men deserve help—they were enslaved; then freed and segregated. Jews suffered greatly when they were segregated. But why affirmative action for women? Is this some kind of political game—are we saying that discrimination against white women is the same thing as discrimination against black men? Statistically, we get the same "utilization" credit for hiring or promoting a white woman as we do a black man. A black woman is a "twofer": one in the black column, a second in the female. That's ridiculous! It's demeaning to black men. It's worse than that—it may deprive a black man of a livelihood and his proper role as breadwinner.

What about priorities? Don't we need to make amends to black men first—shouldn't we start there?

If it were up to me, affirmative action would have been limited to black men. It would have been clearly labeled as reparations for slavery and job discrimination. I would have phased it in over a number of years to make sure that black men were sufficiently educated to take full advantage of the reparations. If I'm competing against 50 million white American men, I can compete against 60 million black and white American men. Once we get used to black men in the work force, and see what kind of society that produces, we can consider whether anyone else needs affirmative action. Affirmative action can't be forever—it is demeaning to the intended beneficiary: did they hire me because I'm good, or because I'm black? Are they hiring me because they want to or because they have to? Do I have to perform well, or is performance irrelevant?

When my mind returned to the affirmative action class, the presentation was just about over. A couple of people had questions. I didn't pay much attention to them, either. It wasn't my job to find affirmative action candidates—the personnel department rounded up the candidates; all I did was interview them. I simply made it a point to tell Personnel the tax function was technically demanding, we had an important responsibility, and I wasn't going to accept anyone who wasn't qualified.

But, for the first time in my life, I wondered whether there was anything I should do about improving the lot of blacks in America.

●　　●　　●

One thing I wasn't going to do was to send our son Eric to public school. I was a product of public schools. So was Toby. But that was when public schools were synonymous with neighborhood schools. My parents made sure I never lived in a neighborhood that lacked outstanding public schools. Once court-ordered busing became the order of the day, as far as I was concerned, the day of the neighborhood school, and the community parental involvement it implied, was over.

It was 1972, and Eric was entering first grade. In our families, educating your children was the highest priority after family survival. One of the concerns Toby and I had when we moved to Winston-Salem was quality public education. Although we did not study the local situation, we had a nagging general concern regarding public education in the South. Once the demise of the neighborhood school was all but assured, we knew we were going to have to find a way to pay private school tuition without Toby finding a job. We did it. We held on to the cars we owned. We delayed the purchase of living room furniture. We retained our 13-inch black-and-white television set and the folding trays we had used as end tables since our marriage in 1963.

In retrospect, the pattern of conspicuous non-consumption we developed during those years became the linchpin of our lifestyle. It also produced some laughs. One visitor to our home inquired whether a completely empty living room was a Jewish custom. We explained it was not; just a personal aversion to installment purchases.

In 1972, we had to make a choice about where Eric should attend school. We chose private non-sectarian. When Eric thrived at Forsyth Country Day, the issue was settled: Eric's brother Steven would attend there as well. We weren't about to sacrifice our children to a court-ordered social experiment.

SEVEN

I t seemed like no time at all before the next annual affirmative action review was upon us. Once again, we were addressed by personnel's EEO compliance officer: "Most of you are familiar with the basic rules, so this year we are going to concentrate on recent legal developments. By way of background, let me remind you that the U.S. Supreme Court, in the case of *Griggs v. Duke Power Company* held ..."

Once again my mind wandered.

How was it possible, after all these years, that blacks hadn't assimilated in America? It's like they're not there—they're invisible. Oh, sure, they're downtown, they're in retail and fast food. But they aren't anywhere I'm doing business—law and accounting firms, corporate headquarters. Some say their education is inadequate, their institutions are weak, they're too dependent on the government—they're not like us. How do we know this? On what are we basing our judgments? We've run away from them—moved away from their neighborhoods. Who do we know—our maids? It is perverse for us to exclude blacks and then to criticize them for not being like us.

In the business world, this is really a catch-22. If every employer hires only experienced people, then no inexperienced person can get a job. I guess we really do need legally mandated affirmative action for blacks.

I'm having trouble looking blacks in the eye when I pass them on the street. I'm so color conscious, and so beset with a case of the guilts. Hell, I didn't invent this world. But what am I doing to change it? And what would I do if I tried? I know life isn't fair. But aren't we obliged to pursue justice?

It wouldn't surprise me if some black men hate white men like me. Whenever I think about race issues I get distracted and can't think about anything else, but I only think about it once in a while. They have to think about it every day.

Once again, the lecture was at an end. And once again, I was troubled by the issue of blacks and whites in America. But not very troubled. Nevertheless, I began to look for opportunities to interact with the local black community.

Looking back, my evanescent interest in the problems of the black community was emblematic of my lifelong empathy with the underdog. Even while seeking to enhance my own status, I was never willing to compromise my visible support of the social and academic misfits in my milieu. But that's the point; at this stage of my life, there were no blacks in my milieu. Nevertheless, I occasionally seized upon perceived opportunities to at least learn a little bit about the black community.

Just such an opportunity presented itself in the late 1970s when I was asked to help fill an R. J. Reynolds sponsored table at a Winston-Salem NAACP fund-raising dinner.

R. J. Reynolds frequently bought a table or two at dinners sponsored by organizations favored by important supporters of the company, particularly customers. I agreed to attend because I was interested in what the featured speaker, Dr. Benjamin Hooks, a nationally recognized civil rights leader and president of the NAACP, might have to say. Institutional fund-raising dinners were variations on a theme. The unusual aspect of this dinner for me was the preponderance of blacks in the audience.

Dr. Hooks's address, as best I remember it, was sort of a State of the Union message from the black perspective, and fairly predictable. I was just about ready to write off the evening as a waste of time when Dr. Hooks said something that got my attention: that the black community needed to do more for itself.

My immediate reaction was one of embarrassment. I felt as if I, a non-family member, had been invited to dinner at which a family argument had resurfaced. I couldn't understand why Dr. Hooks would discuss family business with non-family members present.

Later that evening, it dawned on me that Dr. Hooks' address was memorable for me because it was the first time I had ever heard a black civil rights leader suggest blacks had some responsibility for their own condition. In my mind, I fully agreed black self-help was an essential ingredient in elevating the status of blacks in America.

My visceral belief in the redemptive power of community self-help had been developing for more than a decade, and this increasing awareness was entirely attributable to my growing up Jewish in America.

At age 26, and prior to June, 1967, my view of my Jewish heritage was warped. To me, Judaism was only a religion, and a divided one at that. As a child, I had seen synagogue politics envelop my father in fruitless endeavors. Many German Jews had no respect for Eastern European Jews, coreligionists, and the feeling was mutual. Grown men had argued in a spiteful, arrogant way about what was "Torah true" tradition and custom, and ostentatiously posed as pious and self righteous.

On the social side, things appeared to be no better. American Jews were a minority seen as separate and different. Which came first, involuntary exclusion or voluntary separation, was unclear. Acts of anti-Semitism were clear. Being labeled Christ-killers was clear.

Certain individual Jews were admired and respected. But this was certainly not the case concerning the Jewish people *en masse*. Growing up in Washington, D.C., it was painfully obvious there were places we could not live, firms we could not join, and colleges that had a Jewish quota. The wandering Jew was not necessarily wandering voluntarily. And in the Holocaust of World War II we had irretrievably lost six million, one-third of the world's Jewish population. We were a pariah people.

We were also the butt of jokes. Arthur Goldberg was Secretary of Labor during a portion of President Kennedy's term. The story was told that the president and his cabinet were skiing in the Alps. An avalanche roared down upon the president and his colleagues. Fortunately, by nightfall all were accounted for—except Secretary Goldberg.

The next morning, a rescue party, assisted by Red Cross personnel, set forth to find Goldberg. As the hours passed, the rescue party, sensing a tragedy in the making, called frantically into the snow-covered valley— "Goldberg! Goldberg! It's the Red Cross!" Almost immediately, another voice echoed through the canyon— "I gave at the office!"

Lack of charitable impulse was not the only degradation visited upon Jews by malicious jest. Perhaps the most egregious false accusation masquerading as humor suggested that Jews were cowards who avoided military service. The facts were that Jews had been significant participants as U.S. military personnel in every American war. But facts never stopped those bent upon character assassination, and the myth of martial incapacity was also perpetuated by irreverent humor. The story was told of the Jewish Unknown Soldier: "He was a statesman, a scholar, a teacher—but as a soldier he was unknown."

There was a perceptible fall-off in private humiliations suffered by American Jews following June 5, 1967. The world had watched as President Nasser of Egypt, supported primarily by Syrian and Jordanian forces, and supplemented by troops from Iraq, Algeria, Morocco, Kuwait, and Saudi Arabia, virtually encircled the State of Israel, with the avowed objective of destroying it. On the morning of June 5, the Israelis launched a preemptive strike, sending almost its entire air force of approximately 200 planes to destroy the Egyptian air force. The mission was accomplished in less than three hours. Within one week, Israeli forces had advanced to the Suez Canal and controlled the Jordan River, the Golan Heights and all of Jerusalem.[5,6]

The positive impact on American Jewry attributable to the Israeli victory was palpable. In one week, the world's perception of Jews had turned from one of weakness to one of strength. For those of us who had borne the stigma of perceived weakness, entire new vistas emerged. It was even possible for a non-smoking Jewish Yankee like me to be considered for employment by a manufacturer of tobacco products based in Winston-Salem. I, and most of my American coreligionists, became indebted to the Israelis far beyond our capacity to repay them.

A few years later, I was asked to contribute to the Winston-Salem Jewish Community Council. During that conversation, I learned Israel's defense expenditures represented a huge percentage of its tax revenues. Although my initial pledge was modest, my private commitment to myself was that I intended to assist Israel in meeting its social welfare needs, to the best of my ability, for as long as necessary. As a Jew, I was hardly alone in recognizing both the need and the obligation, and pledging to do my part. That pledge marked my entry into the welcoming arms of the United Jewish Appeal.

During my career in corporate America, I came to realize American business leaders appreciated more than Israel's military strength. They had at least equal admiration for the ability of America's Jews to be self-supporting. "You guys sure know how to raise money" or similar sentiments were expressed to me from time to time, more often than not by people who knew little more about me than that I was Jewish.

Most of the time, the statement was made condescendingly, and elicited from me only the perfunctory "you're right—we sure do." But occasionally, the speaker implied admiration, to which I responded more effusively along the following lines:

"You're right—it's the best thing we do. You call it charity; we call it *tzedaka*. You consider it good, but voluntary; we consider it just, and mandatory. It's a Jewish tax, enforced by peer pressure. We do it primarily because it's right, not just because it makes us feel better. It helps us focus on community needs rather than our own personal needs. In today's world, it's just about all that's left of our claim to being a light unto the nations. As I said, it's the best thing we do."

EIGHT

During the rest of the 1970s, the issue of blacks in America remained a low priority for me, marked only by an occasional urge to "do something." I began to search for black political office seekers whom I could support, and I found a few. One such politician invited Toby and me to attend the wedding of one of his daughters. We accepted.

The wedding, like the NAACP dinner, was unexceptional. It was like most of the weddings I had attended, simply another variation on a theme. But this variation was black. I was supersensitive to being one of the few whites in attendance. And once again, during the course of the ceremony, my mind began to wander.

> Look at this fine young couple. What does life hold in store for them? What are their hopes and dreams and aspirations? When did they become aware that they were black, and that being black mattered? How had their parents discussed the issue with them? What did they suggest? Ignore it? Forget about it? And what are they going to tell their children? And when are they going to tell them? And how are they going to tell them? God, this is so sad. I'm starting to cry—this really hurts. I'll just wipe my eyes, no one will notice. Many people cry at weddings. Do they resent our being here? Maybe they aren't judgmental— after all, we're here, aren't we? We are part of the congregation that is observing their public vow of mutual commitment, and implicitly wishing them all the best and Godspeed.

The service ended. The reception ended. Toby and I retreated to our car. We didn't discuss our thoughts about this very much; we simply agreed we were glad we went. And I quietly hoped for the day when an interracial experience was no big deal either for me or for America.

By the early 1980s, I had become sufficiently visible in the Winston-Salem business community to be invited to join a newly formed Rotary Club. Unlike the downtown club, whose membership included many well-known community leaders, the Rotary Club of Reynolda had few such notables, with one major exception: Clarence E. "Bighouse" Gaines Sr., the nationally known athletic director and basketball coach at Winston-Salem State University. Winston-Salem State was an historically black college whose commitment to excellence had led to its becoming, in 1972, one of 16 constituent institutions of the University of North Carolina.

Coach Gaines was an acknowledged star. In 1961, one of his best players, Cleo Hill, made history when he became the first player from a historically black institution to play professionally in the NBA. In 1967, Coach Gaines and Vernon Earl "the Pearl" Monroe led Winston-Salem State to the NCAA Division II Basketball Championship—the first historically black college to win a national championship. And although it was not knowable at the time, it would come to pass by 1997 that Coach Gaines's record at Winston-Salem State would place him behind only Adolph Rupp at Kentucky and Dean Smith at North Carolina on the roster of most career wins by a college basketball coach.[7]

As I sat at one of our Rotary lunches listening to a fellow Rotarian regale us with autobiographical anecdotes, I drifted once again:

Is there no way that blacks and whites can work together on something? We've got affirmative action in the workplace, but it's mandated by law. Can't we have voluntary affirmative action in our town so we can come together as a community? But how are we going to come together if we don't mix? And how do you even raise the point? I still have almost no black acquaintances, and no black friends. But even if I did, what would it matter? This is a societal issue and no one is talking about it. Everybody knows about it, but nobody talks about it. I wonder what Clarence thinks about all of this? How can I even raise the issue with him in a way that's not condescending? Look at him—a tower of dignity and quiet strength. Is he one of the greatest basketball coaches of all time, or merely one of the greatest black basketball coaches of all time? Does it matter? Does he care?

I need to let Clarence Gaines know that I respect him as a man— that I care about his life. I can't believe this—my eyes are tearing again. This is ridiculous.

Sometime later that year, our Rotary club was considering program options. I recommended we attend a Winston-Salem State basketball game. Some were intrigued; no one objected.

We hired a bus for the evening. Approximately one-third of our membership (about 25 in number) piled on the bus on our side of town for the 15-minute ride to the campus. Clarence had arranged a fine evening for us: dinner on campus; comments from the coach; a few words from some of his players, preceded by the coach's take on each player.

It was obvious even to the casual basketball observers in our midst why Coach Gaines was such a success. Physically, he was the strong, silent type, an imposing giant of a man. My impression was that his success was primarily attributable to his personal qualities. His approach seemed very much dictated by his assessment of the individual strengths and weaknesses of his team and those of his opponent. He was intimately aware of the capacities, predilections and shortcomings of each of his players. He quietly commanded respect, and insisted upon discipline, self-sacrifice and teamwork.

Later, we filed into the field house and sat together somewhere near midcourt. I was somewhat self-conscious about my "alien" status. Was there really any difference between watching two black basketball teams wearing ACC team logos and two black basketball teams representing historically black institutions? Was there really any difference between watching a game at Winston-Salem State and watching a game at the "Dean Dome" in Chapel Hill? Of course there was.

● ● ●

Leadership Winston-Salem was an organization created to provide a cross-cultural experience to selected or incipient community leaders. I was chosen to participate in its year-long program beginning in 1986. For many participants, it represented a networking opportunity. For me, it was an opportunity to meet black community leaders. Each month the group was exposed, through presentations and visitations, to community institutions, services and leaders. Public education, utilities, planning, jails, politics and public safety were all on the agenda.

One program day was devoted to race relations. Ostensibly, the purpose of that day was to facilitate the participant's self-analysis of his own prejudices.

During the course of the day, it became evident most of us felt we didn't have any prejudices. This attitude was best exemplified by the pronouncement made by one of the white participants, a well-known community leader:

> "Let me tell you something. I want to make one point crystal clear. I don't care who moves into my neighborhood. I don't care what their color is, what race they are, what religion they practice. If they can afford the price of a house in my neighborhood, that is the end of it. I'd be pleased to have anyone in this group as a neighbor. Just come on in."

Although I might have been a little less smug about it, as far as I was concerned, that statement pretty well reflected my sentiments on the matter.

In any event, I was unprepared for what followed immediately. One of the black participants indicated his interest in responding. Being duly recognized by the professional facilitator specifically retained for that day's program, the black man responded plaintively, and with barely disguised agitation:

> "Unfortunately, sir, that is not really the point. I am pleased to say to you that I would be equally delighted if you would move into my neighborhood, and become my neighbor. Would you do that?"

The speaker then moved quickly to voice additional concerns about inadequate housing options for upper-middle-class blacks on his side of town, and the need to drive many miles to reach the upscale shopping on our side of town. But I remained fixed on his initial statement. Once again I drifted into thought:

> *I've never even considered that possibility. But I'm thinking about it now. He's right. There is no way I would move into a black neighborhood. Suppose there were only 10 black families out of 25—would I move in then? It depends—if the neighborhood had stabilized, maybe yes. But if it was in transition, probably not. Almost certainly not. Suppose a few black families moved into my neighborhood. Would I move out? How many black families would have to move in before I moved out?*

Many years later, I discovered that my personal musings on the subject, repeated by many white Americans all over the country, constituted one basis for residential segregation by race in America. The Kerner Commission, writing in 1967, described the process in this way:

> "Massive transition" requires no panic or flight by the original white residents of a neighborhood into which Negroes

begin moving. All it requires is the failure or refusal of other whites to fill the vacancies resulting from normal turnover.

Thus, efforts to stop massive transition by persuading present white residents to remain will ultimately fail unless whites outside the neighborhood can be persuaded to move in.

This tiny incident at Leadership Winston-Salem was a revelation. Over the years, I had come to take pride in my maturation, my willingness to absorb new ideas, new people, and new perspectives. I took pride in my new southern heritage, my newfound appreciation of liberal Judaism, my empathy towards Christians, my ability to search for the good in people without being disarmed by naiveté. But at the same time, I failed to either recognize or acknowledge a sad reality: when it came to blacks in America, I was part of the problem. For someone like me, who valued people and humanity above all else, this was a humbling and potentially crippling discovery.

But my thinking had not progressed that far by the mid-1980s. At that point, I had defined my problem differently. My problem was, I decided, I was not doing enough *for* blacks. Well, not to worry; that problem was remediable.

NINE

In August 1986, Toby and I were visiting her family in Boston. I called my secretary in Winston-Salem to check on things.

"Mr. Sidman," she said. "I've got some interesting news. The board voted to put Ross Johnson in as CEO in place of Ty Wilson. Do you think we're gonna be okay?"

"Wow, that is a surprise," I said, stifling my astonishment. "Sure, we'll be fine."

The rest of the conversation was a blur. I closed by reassuring her that I didn't anticipate any drastic changes. I lied. I knew my career at RJR was over. I decided to keep that knowledge to myself.

When I returned to Winston-Salem, I had a chance to reflect a little bit more on the implications for me of Ty Wilson's demise and Ross Johnson's ascendancy.

I had worked with Ty Wilson through major transitions in the company's history, and I liked what I saw. The feeling must have been at least somewhat mutual: Ty had promoted me to senior vice president. In addition, he once approached me about a purely personal matter that meant quite a lot to me—whether I had any interest in joining a country club. He assured me if I had any such interest, he would see to it my admission would be secured without incident. Ty knew his sponsorship of a Jew for membership at one of Winston-Salem's prestigious clubs would not necessarily enhance his corporate image, but he was willing to do it because he thought it was the right thing to do.

I accepted his offer because I thought it was the right thing to do, too. For me, golf was a four-letter word. Growing up, I had always been able to play most sports with a modicum of skill: baseball, football, basketball and tennis. Not so with golf. The game did not come naturally to me, and I had never been willing to devote the time and effort necessary to develop even rudimentary skill. I played tennis twice weekly at Wake Forest University. By all appearances I had no need for any country club memberships.

But I did have such a need. Over the years I had become convinced that the perceived leaders of society established the norms concerning what constituted acceptable behavior in that society. I had further concluded that country club members were among the perceived leaders of American society. It was important to me that the Winston-Salem country clubs not be perceived as sanctioning the exclusion of Jews as acceptable behavior. To my knowledge, Winston-Salem's prestigious Old Town Club did not have one Jewish member. I felt it was important to change that. I accepted Ty's offer, and the membership materialized in due course.

But my incipient relationship with Ty Wilson was made moot by Ross Johnson's election as CEO. I hardly knew Ross, but I knew how he had operated in the past. Ross Johnson had been CEO of Standard Brands when Nabisco acquired it in 1981. By 1984, Ross Johnson was CEO of Nabisco Brands, the combined company, and 21 of the company's top 24 officers were Standard Brands men. I didn't expect things to go any differently at RJR Nabisco.

The purge of the Reynolds executives commenced in the fall of 1986. Fortunately for me, I was not terminated, but my responsibilities were truncated, my title reduced to staff vice president and general tax counsel, and my executive management authority, although limited at best, was eliminated. I had become a corporate eunuch.

The next tremor was felt in early 1987. Unbeknownst to me, Ross Johnson was intent upon moving RJRN's corporate headquarters out of Winston-Salem. As reported incessantly in the local newspaper, Winston-Salem stood accused by Ross of being bucolic.[8] I had never heard the word bucolic used as an insult before.

The rumor mill began working overtime at that point; New York, Dallas, Atlanta. We knew it had to be urban with first-class international transportation.

I was extremely pleased when Atlanta was chosen, for a number of reasons. In the 18 years we had lived in Winston-Salem, I had become a southerner. I resented Yankee caricatures of southern mores. I resented those who considered southern accents to be badges of intellectual inferiority. I resented those who used southerners as scapegoats for their own prejudices. As a Jew, I identified with the southerner as a victim of prejudice. And, as an American, I identified with the burden of the southerner as the cultural descendant of the only Americans to admit to losing a war. I wanted to stay in the South, because it had become my home.

The South was also where Toby and I had come of age as Jews. It took a while, but over the years we adjusted to the organ music, the choir, and prayer in the vernacular. Fortunately, during this period, elements of the Reform movement had moved toward a more "traditional" perspective. More important, it was in Winston-Salem that we discovered the concept of Jewish communal life beyond synagogue worship, and its primacy in our lives.

Jewish communal leadership in Winston-Salem was not in superabundant supply. Those of us who were interested in Jewish communal life had no choice but to become active, and in more than one role. For me, this meant a fair degree of self-study. For the first time, I read published materials on Jewish history, tradition and communal organization, much of which reinforced my belief in self-help as a bulwark against tyranny by the majority.

Toby and I were enthused about a move to Atlanta because it offered us an opportunity to expand our Jewish horizons. Our understanding was the Atlanta Jewish community was special; it offered many of the benefits of a small-town Jewish community combined with the vibrancy that growth provides.

But there was another significant element to Atlanta that intrigued me: the apparent strength of the black community. I wanted to learn more about it. Most of my Winston-Salem based colleagues at RJR Nabisco were chagrined at the thought of leaving Winston-Salem. I was not. If I could do good for blacks in Winston-Salem, think of how much more good I could do for blacks in Atlanta. But first I needed to move there.

We contracted to purchase a home under construction in Fulton County, not too far from the planned RJR Nabisco headquarters in Cobb County. We anticipated a September 1987 move-in date. Figuring it would take us at least four months to sell our home, we placed it on the market in late April. It was sold the day we placed it on the market, and closed in June. We found a small two-bedroom townhouse in Winston-Salem for the summer.

That turned out to be another learning experience for the Sidmans. The four of us shared cramped quarters, nondescript rental furniture, a 13" TV, small crawly creatures, peeling wallpaper, exposed pipes, a slow commode, and pre-Columbian linoleum.

For the first time in our lives, we were going backwards. And we didn't handle it very well. We were curt with one another. Our nerves were frayed.

We began to understand what close quarters and a complete lack of privacy could do to a family.

●　●　●

On the day Toby and I had set for our move to Atlanta, I had made an appointment to meet with Cleon Thompson, the chancellor of Winston-Salem State University and one of my Leadership classmates.

"Arnie," he said, "what are you doing here? If I were moving, I wouldn't come to see you!" He smiled as he spoke the words.

I told him of my interest in working with the black community in Atlanta. "I'll be happy to introduce you to Andy," he responded.

"Thanks, Cleon, but I don't think that's the way for me to go. I really need to meet the people."

"Well," he concluded, "don't hesitate to call on me for help."

What I didn't discuss with Cleon was my recollection of Dr. Hooks' ringing indictment of the black community delivered almost a decade earlier at the NAACP dinner I attended: "We don't do enough for our own." It was this apparent fact of life in the black community I intended to address.[9]

But first I needed to try to get a handle on the black community: its history, its institutions, its capacity for self-help. Reading, I knew, would constitute the bulk of my preparation, but I also knew experiential education was critically important. Woody Allen had been quoted as saying that 90 percent of success in life is attributable to just showing up. I decided to further my quest by just showing up in the black community.

Not long after our move to Atlanta, a dinner honoring Alonzo Crim, the retiring superintendent of Atlanta Public Schools, offered an early opportunity for showing up. Given the demographics of Atlanta's school system, I anticipated a large turnout from the black community.

I was not to be disappointed. The black tie affair, at one of Atlanta's upscale hotels, was well attended. As I gazed around the room, I was taken with the fact that, except for the race of most of the attendees, the dinner was indistinguishable from similar events I had attended over the years. By the end of the evening, I was convinced the strength of Atlanta's black community had not been overstated, and that it had the capacity to implement my idea.

What was my idea? Simply put, it was to encourage black community leaders to create a black community alliance similar to that which had served the American Jewish community so well over the 20th century. The goal of the council would be to protect and advance the political, economic and social welfare agenda of Atlanta's black citizens.

How had I come to this point in my life? Why did I care? What was causing me to embark on a venture that, on its face, was almost certain to be perceived as an affront to the dignity of the intended primary beneficiary? After all blacks had endured in our country, how could I possibly have the arrogance to insinuate myself into black family business? These were the questions I wrestled with as Toby and I settled into Atlanta.

TEN

An obsession has been defined as a persistent disturbing preoccupation with an often unreasonable idea or feeling.

My obsession was, and is, the feeling that America is special. I believe we have the greatest opportunity to be a light unto the nations, but also, in turn, we will squander this opportunity unless the black and white communities fall in step together.

Recognizing an obsession is not particularly remarkable; dealing with an obsession is much more of a challenge.

To say that in 1988 I was almost totally ignorant of facts relevant to my obsession is perhaps a slight overstatement. As was true of most Americans, I was generally acquainted with 19th-century American history—slavery, the Civil War, and Constitutional amendments confirming that blacks were no longer "property." My law school training had also made me aware of the 1896 U.S. Supreme Court case that publicly confirmed that blacks in America were second-class citizens. In *Plessy v. Ferguson*, the question was whether a Louisiana law mandating separate passenger train compartments for blacks and whites was unconstitutional.[10] In holding it was not, the majority held that, although "the object of the [Fourteenth] Amendment was undoubtedly to enforce the absolute equality of the two races before the law, but in the nature of things it could not have been intended to abolish distinctions based upon color, or to enforce social, as distinguished from political equality, or a commingling of the two races upon terms unsatisfactory to either."

Mr. Justice Harlan was a "liberal" in dissent. He disagreed with the majority opinion upholding legal segregation, arguing that it would "keep alive a conflict of races" thereby doing "harm to all concerned." Most tellingly, however, he betrayed his own belief in white supremacy by arguing equality in civil rights certainly did not imply equality in social status:

> The white race deems itself to be the dominant race in this country. And so it is, in achievements, in education, in wealth and in power. So, I doubt not, it will continue to be for all time. . . . Sixty millions of whites are in no danger from the presence here of eight millions of Blacks. . . .

> [The granting of civil rights to blacks does not imply social equality] for social equality no more exists between two races when traveling in a passenger coach or a public highway than when members of the same races sit down by each other in a political assembly, or when they use in common the streets of a city or town, or when they are in the same room for the purpose of having their names placed on the registry of voters, or when they approach the ballot box in order to exercise the high privilege of voting.

My superficial understanding of 19th-century black American history notwithstanding, I recognized that my knowledge of its 20th-century aftermath was essentially nonexistent, and I set out to remedy that deficiency. I started by looking for books to read. Browsing in bookstores had been an enjoyable pastime for years. Now my browsing became focused upon black history and perspectives.

At the outset of my targeted browsing, I was immediately taken by the variety of descriptions employed by booksellers to identify the genre: Black Studies, Afro-American History, African-American History. I was puzzled by one such designation: Black Interests. Was the bookseller suggesting a white person would have no interest in browsing in that section?

It did not take long before my browsing turned into purchasing, which lead to reading. I was hooked: autobiographical works by Frederick Douglass and Booker T. Washington, social commentary by W.E.B. DuBois, essays and historical works by John Hope Franklin and many others. I was saddened by much of what I learned, but my most devastating discovery was a sociological study commissioned by the Carnegie Corporation prior to World War II.

Andrew Carnegie, the steel magnate, had established his Carnegie Corporation foundation in 1911 for the purpose of advancing and disseminating "knowledge and understanding" in the United States and elsewhere. Carnegie had long supported programs for the improvement of black Americans, particularly those suggested by Booker T. Washington, and Carnegie's name had become associated with both the Hampton and Tuskegee Institutes.

The Carnegie Corporation continued similar support following Carnegie's death in 1919. However, by the time of the Great Depression of the 1930s, when black Americans were uniquely pressured, the corporation needed new information upon which to base its support of black interests. Gunnar Myrdal, a respected Swedish social scientist, was chosen to conduct a comprehensive study about blacks in America. The primary reason for his selection (given that all who made the short list were respected scholars) was his presumed objectivity and lack of bias.

The Myrdal study, a collaborative effort of numerous scholars, was completed prior to the end of 1942. It was comprehensive and detailed. Upon its publication in 1944, the *New York World Telegram* concluded that "once in a decade or generation somebody writes a book which should be required reading for every school and college in the land. Such a book is [Myrdal's] *An American Dilemma*."

Myrdal's findings were predictable: that, with notable exceptions, most white Americans still presumed blacks to be inferior, capable of performing menial tasks only, and lower class. Perhaps the most chilling finding of the report is the following:

> If we forget about the means, for the moment, and consider
> only the quantitative goal for Negro population policy, there

is no doubt that the *overwhelming majority of white Americans desire that there be as few Negroes as possible in America.* If the Negroes could be eliminated from America or greatly decreased in numbers, this would meet the whites' approval—*provided that it could be accomplished by means which are also approved.* Correspondingly, an increase of the proportion of Negroes in the American population is commonly looked upon as undesirable. These opinions are seldom expressed publicly. ... But as general valuations they are nearly always present. Commonly it is considered a great misfortune for America that Negro slaves were ever imported. The presence of Negroes in America today is usually considered as a "plight" of the nation, and particularly of the South. It should be noted that the general valuation of the desirability of a decrease of the Negro population is not necessarily hostile to the Negro people. It is shared even by the enlightened white Americans who do not hold the common belief that Negroes are inferior as a race. Usually it is pointed out that Negroes fare better and meet less prejudice when they are few in number. ... All white Americans agree that, if the Negro is to be eliminated, he must be eliminated slowly so as not to hurt any living individual Negroes. Therefore, the dominant American valuation is that the Negro should be eliminated from the American scene, but *slowly.*

Notwithstanding this seemingly grim assessment, Myrdal was nevertheless optimistic about the future for blacks in America:

America feels itself to be humanity in miniature. When in this crucial time the international leadership passes to America, the great reason for hope is that this country has a national experience of uniting racial and cultural diversities and a national theory, if not a consistent practice, of freedom and equality for all. What America is constantly reaching for is democracy at home and abroad. The main trend in its history is the gradual realization of the American Creed.

In this sense the Negro problem is not only America's greatest failure but also America's incomparably great opportunity for the future.[11]

In the late 1980s, I shared Myrdal's optimism, which in my case was based upon my own experience. I had been a member of the board of the Salvation Army Boys Club in Winston-Salem and the vast majority of club members were black. I enjoyed that experience so much I eagerly responded in the affirmative when asked to join the board of the Boys Clubs of Metro Atlanta. I had read of crime and poverty; what I saw and heard were well-disciplined children who had blossomed in the warmth of the clubs. There were concerned parents who made do with very little and sought a better life for their children, and public housing resident leaders who were very much attuned to the needs of their community.

Following our move to Atlanta, I had joined the Atlanta Chapter of the American Jewish Committee (AJC) because its central thesis, that what is good for the Jews was good for America, appealed to me greatly. I soon became aware of AJC's pioneering efforts in intergroup relations and American pluralism. The surprising element to me was the strength of the relationships it had fostered in Atlanta between leaders of the black and Jewish communities. What I had previously read about was contemporary black anti-Semitism; what I saw and heard were bonds of personal friendship between black and Jewish leaders sustained in an atmosphere of mutual respect and a surprising degree of candor.

And yet, as enjoyable and hopeful as these encounters proved to be, they were nevertheless merely peripheral to my immediate quest: to organize a nucleus of black leaders committed to the establishment of a black community alliance.

To this end, I pursued all manner of opportunities to meet black leaders whom I hoped to convince to become organizers of and evangelists for the proposed black self-help umbrella organization. Chance or contrived encounters with black business and professional people were followed by a written invitation from me for lunch "to discuss an idea I have." Most of my invitations were accepted, which I attributed to my use of company letterhead stationery and its implied promise of power. However, on October 20, 1988, my promise of power became publicly suspect. Ross Johnson, by proposing a leveraged buyout of RJR Nabisco, had put the company and my career in play. It was time to implement my "getaway" plan.

ELEVEN

"**W**hy don't you just walk into Lou Gerstner's office, explain what happened when Nabisco took over Reynolds, and ask for your old job back?"

That was the question Toby asked me in March 1989 after Kohlberg Kravis Roberts outbid Ross Johnson's group to acquire RJR Nabisco, then installed Lou Gerstner as CEO in Ross's stead.

"Tobe, it doesn't work quite that way. Plus, my old job doesn't exist any longer. Even if it did, I wouldn't want it. I'm free at last." I chuckled to myself and silently asked Dr. King's forgiveness.

My friend of long standing, Pat Johnson, had called me in the spring of 1988. Pat and I had shared an office as trial attorneys with the IRS Chief Counsel's office in the mid-1960s. Pat had returned to Texas at about the same time I had departed for Winston-Salem. There he helped build the Houston based law firm of Chamberlain, Hrdlicka, White, Johnson & Williams (that's Pat, fourth from the left) into one of the largest and most respected firms in that city.

After bringing one another up to speed on our respective personal lives, Pat came right to the point. "Arnie, you may not yet be aware of this, but our firm opened an office in Atlanta in 1986. If you ever think about leaving RJR, we sure would like you to join us." (In the language of East Texas, where Pat grew up, "we" means "I".)

The Chamberlain firm had a fine reputation as tax law practitioners, with special expertise in tax controversy matters. That kind of practice fit my vision of my future like a glove.

"Pat, that is a most flattering invitation. I'll give it serious consideration."

A year later, the string had run out on my career at RJR Nabisco, and I had become Of Counsel to the Chamberlain firm, to be effective September 1 of that year. I was more than willing to trade cash for time, in order to "pursue other interests," including becoming a catalyst for establishing a black self-help organization.

Over the better part of a year, I had floated the idea with enough black leaders to form a core of at least marginally intrigued people— a couple of elected officials, a banker, some early retirees from IBM, and a few citizens involved in local social service agencies. After a couple of meetings at our home, the group moved the venue to the Woodruff Library at the Atlanta University Center downtown. At each successive meeting, the number in attendance dwindled. Faced with a reasonably clear message, I abandoned that effort. No one called to ask when we were going to get together again.

Undaunted, I chalked up that defeat to the messenger, not the message. I decided to deliver the message in written form.

By then, I had read a number of mainstream histories of blacks in America, and had started delving into sociological studies. Although the selections I read were random, and not necessarily a fair cross-section of analysis and opinion, I was struck by the stridency, sense of urgency and extreme measures offered in some of these discourses.

I was particularly taken with one book I stumbled upon: *The Black Power Imperative—Racial Inequality and the Politics of Nonviolence.*[12] Its author, Theodore Cross, had an "establishment" bio: trustee of Amherst College, graduate of the Harvard Law School, consultant to the Nixon administration on black economic development, and the list went on.

I found his analysis and synthesis of history and human nature particularly enlightening in explaining the predicament faced by black Americans. In particular, he detailed how white Americans had ostracized and kept black Americans in a subordinate role long after the Civil War had ended.

It was not Mr. Cross's analysis, however, that most intrigued me. It was his apparent primary audience: black Americans.

Mr. Cross, an ostensible member of the white power structure, was not only addressing the black community, he was suggesting that black power be mobilized to achieve, through nonviolent means consistent with traditional political action, that community's rightful share of American economic and political power. I was particularly dismayed that his implicit assumption was that unrelenting confrontation with whites, supported by the coercive powers of government, was inevitable if blacks were to achieve their goals.

I was not (and still am not) prepared to accept such an approach. To me, what made America great were shared values, not government imposed mandates. Accordingly, I drafted a proposal to pitch to a few black community leaders in Atlanta, a portion of which read as follows:

- <u>The black community needs to do a better job of cultivating its strengths and advancing its interests: there is no one else to do it.</u>

  - The black community has been led historically by black clergy/political leaders. They have taken the black community as far as their capacities alone will allow. Black business, professional and other economically successful individuals must now assume community leadership roles, with continued assistance and guidance from clerical and political leaders.

  - An entire generation of bright young blacks, the principal beneficiaries of the civil rights struggle, have come of age. It is time for them to assume their proper role as community leaders. Many of them desire to do so. Unfortunately, few of the existing broad-based black organizations view the world as they do; they are leaderless and frustrated.

  - Many successful blacks have deluded themselves into thinking they can escape the negative aspects of their heritage by "mainstreaming." They are wrong. As long as there exists a substantial and growing black underclass, the black middle and upper class will not receive the respect it seeks and deserves.

- The growing economic and political strength of the black community has not been effectively harnessed and tapped. Efforts such as 100 Black Men, as noble and altruistic as they are, are too narrowly focused to make a real difference, given the present magnitude of school dropout, illiteracy, and drug-related issues.

- The <u>entire</u> black community must be motivated to assume active roles in solving the problems existing within the black community and must be educated to understand that black individual success is ultimately tied to black group success engineered by the black community for itself.

- <u>Proposal: Form a black community-wide umbrella organization for the purpose of developing and implementing the black community agenda.</u>

  - Must be supported both financially and programmatically by a significant cross-section of the local black <u>leadership</u>, particularly the black business and professional community.

  - Must be sufficiently broad-based to appeal to essentially the entire affluent black community, regardless of church, fraternal, or political affiliation (or non-affiliation).

  - Must be capable of raising substantial funds (and, ideally, exerting substantial economic and political pressure) in support of the black agenda.

- Must comport itself in such a manner as to address the needs of the black community while simultaneously convincing the white community that it is in the latter's best interest to cooperate in achieving these goals.

- Responsible, in the final analysis, for inculcating within the black community the concepts of self-reliance and self-respect necessary to succeed in a competitive world where Justice for minorities is a never-ending struggle.

Although you might not guess it from the tenor of this excerpt, I was nevertheless well along the way to understanding that it was simply absurd for me to continue deluding myself that any black leader would seriously entertain my proposal, for the simple reason that, possible merit aside, it was impossible to separate the messenger from the message. The phrase "honky jive" came to mind.

Perhaps more to the point, pushing the proposal was no longer my highest priority. I was beginning to overcome my discomfort with black men and women in an intimate setting simply by showing up in the black community. And the more I showed up, the more I felt at ease. I wasn't about to jeopardize these newly forming feelings and relationships by hurling bombast prematurely. I was having too much fun.

My involvement with the Atlanta Black/Jewish Coalition, a forum for intergroup dialogue supported by the American Jewish Committee, afforded me an opportunity to speak at a weekly meeting of the Concerned Black Clergy of Metropolitan Atlanta. The meeting was being held at Paschal's Restaurant, a landmark eatery and gathering place. Concerned Black Clergy had been formed in 1984 to confront the issues of homelessness, but ultimately evolved into a community forum with a wide-ranging agenda.

As I entered the meeting place I was surprised to see a number of non-blacks and non-clergy in the room. The atmosphere was warm and inviting and my remarks were respectfully received.

At the conclusion of the session, I turned to the gentleman nearest me: "Perhaps you can help me: Do you happen to know what the requirements are for membership in Concerned Black Clergy?"

He grinned. "Well, I can tell you this. You don't have to be black. And, you don't have to be a clergyman." Then, as his grin broadened almost imperceptibly, he continued with a slightly lowered voice. "Some say you don't even have to be all that concerned." I was home.

TWELVE

Toby and I enjoyed travel by car in America. We loved it all—the small towns, winding roads, surprising changes in landscape, incidental contacts with our fellow Americans. Armed with our Triple-A tour books, we would motor à la Charles Kuralt just to see and learn. A trip to Montgomery, Alabama might include a visit to the state capitol, the first White House of the Confederacy, and the Scott and Zelda Fitzgerald Museum. Beginning in 1989, such a trip would also include a stop at the Dexter Avenue King Memorial Baptist Church and a side trip to the George Washington Carver Museum and Booker T. Washington's home, both on the campus of Tuskegee Institute.

But, all of these activities, while educational, were shallow and unfulfilling. I was looking for something more engaging.

Since the subject of bridging the gap between blacks and whites was now a constant on my Atlanta area agenda, my conversations with colleagues and acquaintances occasionally moved to that subject. People who approached me for a charitable or political contribution were particularly vulnerable to my assault. "Do you support improved relations between blacks and whites?" "Does your program support black self-help?"

That's how I met Gregory T. Baranco. I was speaking to a Cobb County attorney about my interest in developing a meaningful relationship with members of the black business community. Upon learning of my interest, he offered the following: "You might be interested in meeting Greg Baranco. He's trying to establish a community bank in East DeKalb County. Would you consider investing in such a venture?"

According to the offering circular, First Southern Bank was being organized primarily by a group of successful black entrepreneurs.

Greg Baranco, the bank's chairman, was identified as the owner of a number of auto dealerships whose combined operations "ranked third among auto dealerships on the *Black Enterprise* magazine's 1988 list of the 100 largest black owned companies in the United States."

A few weeks later, Toby and I were meeting with Greg Baranco and a couple of other organizers of First Southern Bank. We liked what we heard. We liked what we saw. We made a modest investment.

The annual meeting of stockholders was held at the Big Miller Grove Baptist Church in Lithonia. I decided to attend one. As customary at such events, the proceedings were unremarkable, with Chairman Baranco noting steady progress coming along as according to plan.

By this point in my life, most of the symptoms of the Sidney Syndrome of my high school days had dissipated. The cumulative effect of numerous meetings with black individuals and groups, coupled with just "showing up" in the black community, had eliminated my initial discomfort. But I still had not shaken my super-sensitivity to black and white.

So while I felt somewhat comfortable sitting on a folding chair in the basement of "Big Miller" church, I was nevertheless aware that virtually all of those seated around me and around the room were black. And I was white. Why did it matter? Why should it matter? All I knew was that it still mattered, at least to me.

I knew something else, too. I had been a modest investor in any number of ventures; I rarely attended stockholder meetings. But I knew it was very important to me that the black Americans associated with the First Southern Bank see me sitting in that church basement. I wanted to be seen sharing in the risks of the venture, supporting the effort and hoping for its success, and staying for a cup of coffee following the meeting.

I hung around for a few extra minutes following the meeting. I reintroduced myself to Greg and asked if he'd be willing to meet me for lunch.

I still could not let go of the idea that the black community agenda could be advanced by a unified broad-based self-help organization spearheaded by black business leaders. In my *ad hoc* meetings with various black leaders, the rejectionists (a clear majority of those to whom I had put the proposition) fell into two camps. Those who had become adults prior to the zenith of the civil rights movement could not even entertain the idea: "Arnie, I can't conceive of that happening. We're just not used to operating that way." One of the younger skeptics had a different rationale: "Arnie, we can't agree on anything. And we really don't trust one another."

At lunch, I briefly laid the concept on Greg Baranco. "Do me a favor, will you? Read the proposal. Let me have your reaction."

Greg Baranco was the kind of man who could make the proposal a reality.

Weeks went by—no reaction. I finally reached him by phone. "Yes, I've read it. Sure, just get on my calendar, come on over to the office and we'll talk."

When I arrived at his office, he invited me to be seated. "Without going into a lot of detail, let me just say that my preference is to attack the issues you are addressing as a total community. I've always worked on community issues with both blacks and whites. I've always had both black and white employees. I've always had both black and white customers. That's the way I like to do business. Besides, our community has historically provided for our needs through our churches. These roots are broad and deep. I don't see how we could set up any kind of community organization of the kind you are suggesting without recognizing the centrality of our churches."

I bit my tongue. As I was about to leave, he threw me a bone. "Juanita thinks there might be something to it." That was no small bone. Juanita, Greg's wife, was a recognized power in her own right.

About a year went by. Out of the blue, I received an unexpected phone call. "Mr. Sidman, this is Ted Pryor. I'm working on a manuscript that I hope to have published. Juanita Baranco suggested you might be able to help me."

When we finally got together, I discovered that Ted Pryor was a black visionary with a keen sense of world history, a clear preference for "black" (rather than "African-American"), and a strong advocate of black self-help. Ted had retired as an executive with Aetna Life in Hartford, Connecticut. While in Hartford he formed the Ebony Business League, which supported a variety of black self-help efforts. His program achieved such visibility that he invited President Nixon to address the League. Ultimately, Nixon declined.

Ted's manuscript was fascinating. Black capitalism, communal investment strategies, and a monument and museum honoring black achievement in America were among his proposals, all to be financed initially by donations from the black business and professional establishment. Other chapters depicted heroic stories of blacks in America, and a defense of the strategies, role and politics of Booker T. Washington in his early 20th-century debate with W.E.B. DuBois. It wasn't my proposal—it was far grander, soaring and magnificent. It was to be national in scope; a bridge too far, I thought.

"This is just terrific, Ted. My own view is that you can't just go national. You need to develop a working model locally, then spin it out. But I'll do what I can to help you get your manuscript published. Keep one thing firmly in mind. I'm a tax lawyer. I don't know the first thing about getting a book published."

Unbeknownst to Ted, I was also contemplating writing a manuscript and trying to get it published. Stymied by the failure of my black self-help proposal to get to first base, I had decided to take another tack.

THIRTEEN

By the mid-1990s, I had come to some tentative but specific conclusions about issues between blacks and whites in America. To me, whites as a group were being unfairly maligned as racists or white supremacists. Undoubtedly, some whites were still deservedly charged, but most were not. Instead, what I was observing was a pervasive white discomfort in our dealings with the black community. This discomfort was made manifest in numerous ways with a central theme: white flight. We fled central cities and maintained residential segregation. We abandoned the public schools and converted them into jobs programs. We looked the other way as government jobs and transfer payments were expanded beyond control. We congratulated ourselves by our continuing commitment to black civil rights, affirmative action, and guaranteed black political representation. And we continued our longstanding tradition of *noblesse oblige* by providing for our poor black citizens through various acts of charity.

As a Jew, this discomfort scenario was one I had previously witnessed first-hand. Over the decades following World War II, overt anti-Semitism visited upon American Jews by our non-Jewish fellow citizens slowly evaporated, and was reduced to a small but dangerous nucleus of Jew-haters following Israel's victory in the Six-Day War. For the rest of our fellow citizens, any latent anti-Semitism was simply replaced by varying degrees of discomfort (or adopting Israel as a rhetorical proxy). This discomfort also manifested itself in a variety of ways, some of them quite humorous.

During my first few months at R. J. Reynolds in the late 1960s, I was introduced from time to time to senior managers at the company. During some of the ensuing conversations, a number of these managers asked me whether I knew or had met Rouben Chakalian. I responded in the negative. A couple of years later, I was in Geneva, Switzerland, where I was introduced to Rouben for the first time. When I asked whether he could explain this unusual sequence, he responded in the affirmative. "They think I'm Jewish. I'm not. I'm Armenian."

My outsider perspective gave me at least a basic empathy with black Americans and some minimal insight into their predicament. Through no fault of their own, they were under extraordinary pressure to survive in a seemingly very hostile environment. Under such circumstances, you grab what you can—any way you can. And white America looked the other way. Whether from guilt, or fear, or indifference, or whatever, we lowered our standards, first for blacks and then for ourselves.

I had been in the "indifference" group. I was so focused on my career and family I stopped paying attention to what was going on in our country. Getting bounced out of corporate America cured me of this. I was upset at what I saw: irresponsible behavior was everywhere—professional politicians apparently believing they were leaders with answers; entertainers apparently believing their talents gave validity to their vacuous opinions; demands for cheap labor making a mockery of our border controls and citizenship.

One of the most glaring examples of irresponsible behavior was occurring right in my adopted home state of Georgia and was being hailed nationally as a political master stroke. The Hope Scholarship promised full tuition and more to Georgia's university system for any Georgia high school graduate with a B average. The scholarship was financed by a Georgia state lottery, and was not limited only to those whose families needed the money. Here we had the perverse policy of state-sponsored gambling for people who could ill afford the losses subsidizing the college educations of the children of affluence. To add insult to injury, grading by teachers, which had been inflated for years as a misguided boost to self-esteem, now took on a much more serious dimension—a child deprived of a B average might be denied a college education of worth. Even the most principled teacher might buckle under the weight of that decision.

FOURTEEN

T ed Pryor opened my eyes to an entire new world. He introduced me to lesser-known black historical figures. He explained why, in his opinion, blacks needed their own religion. He invited me into his home. He and his wife Sophornia invited Toby and me to the annual Sigma Pi Phi Christmas dinner dance.

Sigma Pi Phi was not one of the myriad black undergraduate social fraternities. It was a fraternity of the black elite, men who had achieved significant success in their chosen fields. According to the evening program:

> The Sigma Pi Phi Fraternity was founded May 15, 1904, in Philadelphia, Pennsylvania, and is the oldest African-American fraternity of [educated, professional] men in the world. The Boul[é] [affiliate] in Atlanta was initiated in 1920 and was called the Kappa Boul[é].

> The fraternity's organizational structure mirrors [social structures of] Greek history and tradition. In ancient Greece, the boul[é] was an advisory council of elders. All members of boul[é]s in Sigma Pi Phi Fraternity are called "Archons," a Greek term for chief magistrate. Emphasis in the fraternity is placed upon education, professional achievement, family, and the family association. In Sigma Pi Phi an Archon's wife is a very important part of the Boul[é] Society; she has the designated revered status of "Archousa." The Archons of Kappa Boul[é] believe Christmas is for the Archousai. We invite you to celebrate with us.

Toby and I were honored to have been invited.

Ted and I had already gotten to know one another quite well before the evening of the party. Unfortunately, his comfort zone with me did not extend to the rest of the attendees. There was no conversation with me that I did not initiate. The responses were terse and limited to the question asked. Cool and indifferent was my take on the reaction of the crowd to our presence.

One attendee, however, was neither cool nor indifferent. I had just ascertained he was a senior official at one of the colleges historically attended exclusively by black students.

"That's quite interesting," I said. "So, how are things on your campus?" What a great question I had posed. Open-ended, showing interest in the other guy's life. And delivered with one of my better Mr. Sincerity smiles.

"We'll survive," said he. "Of course, we wouldn't need any of these schools if you treated our kids better." If scowls could kill, I would have been a dead man.

About two years later Toby and I attended a Bar Mitzvah reception. About an hour into the dancing, shortly after the *hora*, the band leader announced, with great enthusiasm, "Ladies and gentlemen, we have a special treat for you this evening. We're going to teach you a brand new dance that's the latest craze, the Electric Slide!" I didn't do old dances, much less new ones, but I was nevertheless intrigued. As I watched the lines being formed, and as the instructor began to walk and talk through the steps, I began to grin knowingly. I had seen this dance before, performed beautifully and without instruction, by the Archons, Archousa and guests of the Kappa Boule Chapter, Sigma Pi Phi fraternity, at their Annual Christmas Celebration.

●　●　●

Even though I had struck out with Greg Baranco, I couldn't let my black self-help agenda go without one more try.

Through my Boys and Girls Clubs contacts, I had been introduced to Owen Montague, who turned out to be the driving force behind the Atlanta Exchange, an umbrella organization of more than 25 black business and professional organizations whose combined memberships then exceeded 3,000 individuals. Lawyers, doctors, accountants, secretaries, general contractors—all were represented by their respective trade or professional organizations. The primary thrust of the Exchange was black business networking, but I hoped to convince Mr. Montague to expand its reach to include a broader self-help agenda. I struck out once again.

In the meantime, I continued to be troubled by the issue of blacks and whites in America. To me, the whole discussion had taken on an *Alice In Wonderland* quality. We focused on black crime, but took solace in the fact that most black perpetrators victimized black individuals. We were preoccupied with the breakdown of family values in the black urban ghetto without wondering if we were at all implicated in the misfortune. We separated ourselves from them, then complained they did not act like us. We insisted the world know and remember the Holocaust of European Jewry. But we were almost silent concerning what our own citizens, much less the world, should know about our role in black slavery, Jim Crow, exclusion of our black citizens from whole areas of our society, and the contributions of black Americans to the commonwealth in spite of these conditions, barriers and slights.

We could not understand how Israelis in West Jerusalem and Palestinians in East Jerusalem could live so close together and yet live so far apart. Yet we failed to see the relevance of that observation to describe our own black and white urban condition. We took pride in residing in cities "too busy to hate," as if such an accomplishment were praiseworthy. We rightfully prided ourselves on our freedom, while being fearful of entering large portions of our own cities.

Finally, we argued about the merits of legally imposed affirmative action without asking whether we were capable of instituting some voluntary form of such action which might be both morally superior to, and more consistent with our basic values, than mandatory preferential treatment.

FIFTEEN

Many years ago, an apocryphal story percolated among American Jews that can help to elucidate the issue of black-white relations. It was told that one Murray Bender (formerly Bendikoff) had become a successful businessman. Murray was the first child born in America of immigrant parents from Eastern Europe, the "old country." Murray's parents had spoken broken English, liberally sprinkled with Yiddish, all their American lives.

Murray was a yachtsman. He desired to join the local yacht club. He wanted the facilities, amenities and business contacts that club membership would bring. More than that, he wanted the social status attributed to club members.

An acquaintance of Murray's learned of his interest and offered to submit his name for membership. A few months later, Murray received a call from this acquaintance. "Murray, I've got some bad news. This yacht club membership is a little more complicated than I thought. I'll keep you posted."

During the ensuing years, Murray and the acquaintance spoke to one another from time to time. The yacht club membership was never discussed.

Then one day, Murray answered the phone. "Murray, I've got good news for you. Your yacht club membership is in the bag. I'll mail you the application. Just send it in."

Murray was elated. In due course, he became a member in good standing of the yacht club.

Parental approval had been important to Murray all his life. So, one Sunday in June, he invited his parents to accompany him to the club. Murray was all decked out for the occasion; double-breasted blue blazer, white ducks, nautical chapeau, the works. After touring the club, Murray and his parents boarded his boat.

There stood Murray, proud as a peacock, surveying the port scene, the other boats glistening in the harbor, his parents at his side. He turned to his mother.

"Well, Mama, what do you think of your captain now?"

"Oy, *mein kind*, by me, you're a captain. And by Papa, you're a captain. But what are you by the captains?"

When I first heard this story, I grinned at what I perceived to be its principal and subsidiary reminders. The latter was simple: in the field of human relations, mother knows best.

The former was somewhat ambiguous. My first take was that Murray was simply being gently reminded not to forget that he was a Jew. In later years, though, I began to see facets of the story that had previously escaped me.

Murray is not a fool. He has changed his name in part because he is living in a time in America when he perceives his Jewish-sounding name to be a net liability. He is a successful businessman. However, he wants to be more than just a successful businessman; he wants the trappings and esteem that go with it. He wants respect.

Now he is a member of the prestigious club. He is a member in good standing. He is a holder of a certificate evidencing this fact, and setting forth that as such he is entitled to enjoy all the "benefits and privileges appurtenant thereto." He is entitled to vote and to exercise all of the civil rights available to members in good standing. Is he entitled to get a second Jew into the club? How about a third? Does he care? Should he care?

And what about respect? He's a member in good standing. He's got his civil rights. Does it matter to Murray whether the "captains" think of him as Murray the member rather than Murray the Jew?

What about the "captains"? Do any of them think about Murray or any of these questions? Why should they? They have enjoyed the club and its amenities for many years before Murray became a member. As long as Murray abides by the rules, they don't even have to talk to him.

Suppose it really is important to Murray what the captains really think about him. Suppose his need for respect from his peers is palpable and affects his daily life—his drive and determination, his willingness to work hard, to assert himself, to take risks. What can Murray do about what the captains think and how they treat him?

Well, Murray can invite each of them to his home and try to ingratiate himself with them. How about dinner out? How about throwing a big party at his home, or at a big hotel, or even at the yacht club, where he can not only attempt to ingratiate himself with the captains, but also display his wealth and couth demeanor? And, as the *piece de resistance*, at the end of the evening, Murray, following his Shakespeare reading, can offer to donate $10,000 to each of the captains' designated charities.

At the end of the day, the ultimate tragic message of the Murray story is not that Murray, try as he might, cannot escape the fact that he is a Jew. It is instead the stark reality that there is *absolutely nothing* Murray can do to command the respect of the captains. The respect of the captains is a potential gift that each captain can choose to grant or withhold as he sees fit.

Is a happy ending possible for Murray? How many captains must bestow the token of respect? And in what manner? How many captains were aware of the unwritten exclusionary rule? How many captains were aware of Murray's application process? How many Germans living in Germany during World War II were aware of the forced relocation of their Jewish neighbors and the confiscation of their property?

Does the Murray story matter? I mean, after all, it's only a club.

❂　❂　❂

What about America? Is America a club, or is it something else?

I would suggest that America is not a club, but rather a team. And without putting too fine a point on it, I would suggest further that two key attributes distinguish one from the other. Club members are normally chosen by representatives of the membership, and substantial enjoyment of club benefits is usually guaranteed by simple compliance with club rules. On the other hand, on real teams, team members are usually not able to select their own teammates and team goals are rarely achieved without teamwork.

A contest has been defined as a struggle for superiority or victory. In one sense, then, life is a contest. But is it a contest between individuals, or rather a contest among teams?

For many years, baseball has been an American allegory for life, a national pastime that reflects the American view of what the game of life is all about. Individual effort and capability are key: you must be able to throw, catch, hit and run on your own. No one can help you do these things. Each player on the field is visible and accountable, and responsibility is almost always known or knowable.

But the game requires something more than the actions and abilities of the individual—what about teamwork? After all, players on a team are not only competing with other teams—they are competing with their own teammates as well: for money, for playing time, for respect or adulation. How do they reach their individual goals? And what about team goals—do the individual players care about team goals, or do they just care about individual goals?

Players understand the covenant between the individual and the team. Each individual must contribute to team success. When the individual is faced with a personal difficulty, he has the right to expect his teammates and his team to come to his aid. But no individual has the right to expect his teammates or his team to carry him indefinitely.

Who is responsible for team success?

At first blush, team management seems to be responsible. Management hires the personnel. And management sets down uniform rules of conduct and policy, and penalties for non-conformity. The team manager normally determines who plays, who practices, and who receives coaching or discipline. But none of this necessarily determines success.

What about the intangibles: the drive, determination and grit, all applied over a season or a career, that make the great players great, mediocre players better, and produce winning teams? What about team spirit, the quintessential intangible, which impels individuals to sacrifice self-interest for the good of the team?

My experience tells me it is usually the players, rather than management, that produce the intangibles that separate winners from losers. Teamwork and team spirit cannot be created or enforced by team rules. These attributes of team success can only be achieved through voluntary commitment. Even team standards cannot be enforced solely by team rules. The 55-mile-per-hour speed limit is unenforceable when most of the players wish to exceed it. Mass disobedience trumps the rule of law. Voluntary commitment, not mandated rules, determines team success.

How do players who value team success implement their value system? Styles vary, of course, but at bottom these players make the same decision: we may not have chosen to be with one another, but here we are—I'm going to give my best and I ask that you do the same. Your success has now become my own. What you do with your personal life is your business so long as it doesn't hurt our team. You're my teammate, and I'm going to do what I can to help you—I hope you'll do the same.

Real advantages accrue when the game of life is viewed as a team game. Each player is accountable not only for his or her individual performance, but each team member bears some responsibility for team success. If you're my teammate, I can make reasonable demands for your support of team values and standards. If you're not my teammate, I can make the same demands, but without the leverage that mutual commitment and conscience provide. As your teammate,

I have a commitment to you and your welfare that transcends that which I may feel toward you simply because you're a player.

What has any of this to do with blacks and whites in America?

Simply put, I view our country as Team America, a competitor in the major league game of life. In 1776, when we granted ourselves a franchise, blacks were not considered to be on the team. The 1857 decision of the U.S. Supreme Court in *Dred Scott* did not *deny* team membership to blacks; it merely confirmed the fact that blacks were not considered to be part of Team America.

Shortly thereafter, we engaged one another in a great Civil War for the primary purpose of determining whether we were going to be just one team, or rather two. As a consequence of victory, the victors demanded black Americans be issued team uniforms. There was no requirement they be issued gloves or bats, or treated as teammates.

It was not until after World War II that team management demanded black Americans be issued gloves and bats. Management also demanded black Americans be inserted in the line-up. There was still no requirement that black Americans be treated as teammates, nor could there be.

In my view, white Americans have much to gain by convincing themselves and all Americans that black Americans are our teammates and by treating them accordingly.

Over the years, we have come up with any number of reasons why blacks don't belong on our team. But at bottom, these reasons boil down to one false charge: they cannot play the game of life on our level.

SIXTEEN

G unnar Myrdal, in his seminal work cited previously, quoted the
following statement written by a black scholar in 1931:

> The patronizing attitude is really more damning than the
> competitive struggle. The stone wall of calm assumption of his
> inferiority is to the Negro a keener hurt and a greater obstacle
> than the battle which admits an adversary worth fighting
> against. It is hard to keep ambition alive and maintain morale
> when those for whom you have fondness and respect keep
> thinking and saying that you are only children, that you can
> never grow up, that you are cast by God in an inferior mold.

Myrdal, acknowledging the accuracy of the scholar's implicit
complaint, offered the following insight as to how ordinary white
people came to this belief:

> Race is a comparatively simple idea which easily becomes
> applied to certain outward signs of "social visibility," such as
> physiognomy. Explanations in terms of environment, on the
> contrary, tax knowledge and imagination heavily. It is difficult
> for the ordinary man to envisage clearly how such factors as
> malnutrition, bad housing, and lack of schooling actually deform
> the body and the soul of people. The ordinary white man cannot
> be expected to be aware of such subtle influences as the denial
> of certain outlets for ambitions, social disparagement, cultural
> isolation, and the early conditioning of the Negro child's mind
> by the caste situation, as factors molding the Negro's personal-
> ity and behavior. The white man is, therefore, speaking in good

faith when he says that he sincerely believes that the Negro is racially inferior, not merely because he has an interest in this belief, but simply because he has seen it. He "knows" it.[13]

I have quoted Gunner Myrdal's analysis here because it describes the man I was with reasonable accuracy: I was the ordinary white man of whom Myrdal spoke. Growing up in Washington, D.C., I had passed through black neighborhoods often enough to "know" inferiority when I saw it. On those few occasions when I actually heard a black person speak, it was obvious to me from my inability to clearly understand what was being said I was listening to the speech of an "inferior" being. As I aged, the blacks I met who failed to fit my perception of blacks were seen by me as "exceptions." Over time, it dawned on me the vast majority of blacks I met were exceptions.

Nevertheless, I had come to the realization that black inferiority was a myth only after years of reading about the black experience in America and meeting face to face with a critical mass of black Americans. Most of my white teammates had no such experiences, and what they "knew" simply reinforced the myth: media reports of black crime were a staple of the eleven o'clock news, and black student achievement on standardized tests continued to trail that of their white peers, even after decades of affirmative action. I had already discounted the test results, rationalizing that relative group scores reflected non-measureable factors such as how important success on the test is to the group and how hard the group is willing to work to perform well on the tests, which would be strongly influenced by group experiences in dealing with life and the perceived rewards, if any, associated with education and study. But I also knew that until black academic achievement was perceived to be improving, the chances of true black success in America were likely to be remote.

● ● ●

If life is a team game and we are Team America, it is pertinent to consider how our team is doing. To me, this means unraveling the web of race relations in our past and present in order to play more effectively in the future.

In 1997, Stephan and Abigail Thernstrom co-authored *America In Black and White*, which, according to the publisher, "is the first comprehensive work since Myrdal's to look at the status of African Americans and ask, what has happened and why?"[14] (Apparently, the study of blacks in America is a Scandinavian cottage industry.)

The thrust of the Thernstroms' thesis is that blacks in America have made such great strides since the end of World War II that legally mandated, race-based affirmative action in education, employment and government contracts is not only no longer necessary but has become counter-productive. I wish this view was more widely held by my black American teammates. The Thernstroms' optimism apparently springs in part from their conclusion that white Americans rate high by international standards of intergroup tolerance.

Two concepts implicit in this conclusion trouble me: the measure and the standard. I do not believe the standard should be international, or even western European, because weak competition does not challenge one to perform exceptionally. Further, I do not believe the measure should be tolerance, which in matters of human relations should be relegated to a fallback position.

For those who consider the United States of America just another country, an international standard of tolerance may suffice. But for me, it does not speak well of the potential this country holds. Whether by the grace of God, or historical accident, or both, we now have a unique opportunity to show the world, by our actions, how the game of life should be played. A large part of that opportunity relates to enhancing the quality of relationships between blacks and whites—and on so many levels. But matters of teamwork—of trust, responsibility, and the recognition of value—must come first.

SEVENTEEN

I t is difficult for an American to understand why Quebec, La Belle Province, is forever threatening to separate itself from the rest of Canada.

Canada is almost universally recognized as an outstanding country. Even Canada's populace, both English- and French-speaking, overwhelmingly affirms that Canada is a great place to live. But the problems of Quebec are both complex and simple. The former deals with political power, leverage, and opportunism; with culture, language, and religion; and with history and memory. The latter deals with respect.

The Quebec license plate proclaims *"Je me souviens"*—"I remember."

French-heritage Quebecois remember their ancestors' defeat by the British in 1759. French separatists are dissatisfied as one of 10 co-equal Canadian provinces—they see themselves as one of two co-equal founders, French-speaking Catholics and English-speaking Protestants, of the Canadian federation in 1867. But mostly they remember the lack of respect and patronizing attitude visited upon them by the English-speaking majority.

It is in the realm of disrespect that the complex dissolves and the simple is revealed. People abhor being treated disrespectfully. It makes them angry and resentful. In Quebec, one of the ways Francophiles vent this anger is to threaten, from time to time, to secede from Canada.

I first became aware of this tug-of-war in the mid-1970s. I had been dispatched to Montreal to work on a proposed acquisition of a Canadian enterprise. To assist us in this process, we had engaged a large international accounting firm with offices in Montreal. As I reviewed the scope of the engagement with one of the firm's partners, he seemed bewildered and became taciturn. As a representative of a well-known American company, I had come to expect outstanding performance from firms eager for our repeat business. Finally, he came to the point: "You see, sir, the weight of our prior engagements is such that, in order to meet your timetable, we have no choice but to have this engagement headed by a Frenchman. I am sorry, but there is no alternative. I hope you understand."

The "Frenchman" turned out to be both competent and delightful.

I am no longer surprised by the magnitude of the vote favoring separation of Quebec from the rest of Canada. The most recent vote was cast at the end of October 1995. Almost 50 percent voted for separation. Three days before the vote, tens of thousands of Canadians from every province descended upon Montreal to entreat the Quebecois to remain in the union. But Quebec's separatist leader, Lucien Bouchard, declared Quebec would not be taken in by such a bogus display of government-subsidized affection.[15]

I remind you of the Canadian experience simply to underscore how difficult it is to discern the depths of animosity and despair harbored in the psyche of a people who feel oppressed and ostracized.

Make no mistake—blacks in America feel ostracized. I do not pretend to fully understand the depth of their particular feeling, but, as a Jew, I understand ostracism. And this feeling of ostracism, produced in part by me and by millions of my indifferent and fearful fellow Americans, has induced a state of national paralysis that threatens the very core of our values and dreams.

Think about a baseball team that is playing reasonably well, but is doing so against competition that is mediocre at best. Aside from winning, the players are not having nearly as much fun as they could be having if the team were not beset with occasional dissension and rancor.

Team management is ambivalent. Management has issued numerous directives requiring team members to work together. But, for the most part, these directives are unenforceable. Not only that, management has derived some real benefits from the dissension, as fans pour through the turnstiles to witness the hostility. Media covering the team are also enjoying the benefits of team dissension—newspaper sales have never been higher as fans scramble to keep up with the latest confrontation. Vendor sales are up; T-shirts sport the latest invective in support of rival antagonists and factions.

In fact, for the most part, the only victims of the dissension are the members of the team. The joy of arriving at the ballpark, practicing, and playing, has vanished. The fun is gone.

When this happens to a team, there is only one proven remedy to eradicate the dissension and make playing fun and productive. Self-selected "leaders in the clubhouse" must persuade their teammates, through appeals to reason, cajolery, intimidation, and the like, to desist from their behavior, for the good of the team and their own well-being.

You might ask, what does a remedy for a baseball team of 25 to 40 players have to do with Team America, a team with more than 300 million players?

In principle, the remedy is equally applicable. Team America is comprised of individual competitors living in communities. Some of these communities are small, others huge and ill-defined; but within each are community leaders capable of providing a vision and the means to implement the vision. Only the inclination or will of such leaders is problematic.

What might that vision be? First, the vision would be neither uniform nor universal. In recognition of the truism that all politics are local, the vision would be tailored to the needs and capacities of each community. The goal would be to enhance collective happiness and prosperity by enhancing community capacities and reducing their tensions and fears.

A critical element of the vision would be a profound public acknowledgement of the simple fact that black Americans are our teammates. Scoff if you will, but the chasm between blacks and whites is wide, the road uncharted and strewn with mines of mistrust and cynicism.

"Profound" in political terms implies a sustainable broad base of willing, not grudging, support. The acknowledgment must be actively engaged in voluntarily by a substantial number of adult community residents over a protracted time frame. Participation by paid or elected community proxies will not suffice. Participation by children of community residents will not suffice.

"Public" in political terms implies both visibility and mass involvement. All over America there are private meetings or "dialogues" between blacks and whites. But in political terms, such gatherings are not public; they have essentially no impact beyond those participating. One man marching alone is inconsequential; one man marching in the company of 999,999 others makes a statement; 1,000,000 men marching together daily creates a norm.

Dialogue is clearly a critical part of the vision. But initiated by whom? To discuss what?

Local self-selected community leaders—"leaders in the clubhouse"—must initiate the conversations. In small communities, a few phone calls and some meetings at the general stores might suffice to initiate community-wide potluck "dinners of dialogue" among large numbers of community residents. In larger metropolitan areas, a substantially greater effort, involving a commitment to mobilize volunteers on a scale associated with hosting the Olympics, would be required.

What of the subject matter of the discussions? In the broadest sense, it would be determined by the participants. Hopefully, many potential participants would recognize the endeavor as an opportunity not only to bond with neighbors and others in their existing social milieu, but also to discuss important issues of the day. But, in the final analysis, substance would be secondary. The act of coming together would be primary. The thrust of the effort would simply confirm that white Americans and black Americans are teammates with common life goals.

Man is by nature a social animal. So, in the competition that is life, men have formed teams. Individual accomplishment is prized, but individual victory, while possible, is hollow. Shared joy is sweet.

But shared joy is not possible among teammates who do not share. Sharing requires volition.

EIGHTEEN

This proposal is no pipe dream. Our ancestors have already done the heavy lifting: discovery and colonization of the land, creation of an independent nation, development of a living constitution, territorial expansion and settlement, defense of the new nation, preservation of the union, and in this century, preservation and expansion of our freedoms through politics and war.

We must always remain vigilant regarding threats to our nation from abroad. A nation that is incapable of defending its citizens and the integrity of its borders is disadvantaged in the game of life. Equally important is ensuring that what occurs within its borders is worth the price of that defense.

Make no mistake: what occurs within our borders is highly competitive, among individuals, firms, associations—in literally every field of human endeavor. It is all well and good to speak of love and compassion for our fellow man, but personal survival, which is inherently competitive, is paramount. We measure the results of that competition in a variety of ways: wealth acquired and dispensed, and awards and honors received.

But in the realm of *residential* competition among towns, cities, and regions, the measures of success are usually subsumed within the rubric "quality of life." In the competition among communities for economic and social success, community leaders point with pride to clean streets and air, short commutes, good schools, an airport, and other amenities. Sooner or later, community leaders are going to explicitly recognize racial climate as a significant element of quality of life.

Picture this. It is the year 2020. An award is being presented to Joe Civic on the occasion of his retirement after years of loyal

service to the local Chamber of Commerce as a business recruiter.
After accepting the award, Joe delivers his prepared remarks:

> Thank you all so much. I really appreciate this honor. And it's
> been fun—it really has. But I can't accept this award solely for
> myself. It's been a team effort—a total community effort.
>
> I've been asked to reflect on my years as a downtown devel-
> opment professional.
>
> I well remember my earliest years in this business. Our main
> concern was to revitalize downtown, what they called the
> "inner city" in those days. We had plenty of problems then, at
> least that's the way we saw it. Our metropolitan area was grow-
> ing, but downtown was stagnating. The only people on the
> streets after office hours were tourists, panhandlers or home-
> less. Actually, there wasn't much reason to be downtown at
> night; there was little happening.
>
> It was clear to us that the only way to rejuvenate downtown was
> to encourage people living in the suburbs, and people looking for
> housing generally, to move to downtown. There was a general
> feeling that we could make it happen if we could just get people
> comfortable about coming downtown. We already had some
> developers interested, and a few urban pioneers were there as well.
>
> I don't recall exactly how we got started on the proposal, but
> we began to list the problems people saw—crime, drugs, poor
> schools, dilapidated housing, homeless people—and it just
> seemed overwhelming.
>
> Those of us who had already been playing this game awhile
> knew that we had to add one other problem to the list. We

knew that the key to downtown was residential integration—blacks and whites living together. Oh, we recognized that we had a growing Asian and Latin American population, but the consensus was that time would take care of integrating those populations just as it had for earlier immigrants.

Anyway, we started batting around how it could all be done. Of course, we had some areas where blacks and whites lived together already, so we polled those people to find out what they liked and disliked about their neighborhoods. I remember one thing we learned—people said they didn't know their neighbors. They knew the soccer team parents and some people they saw every week at church, but that was about it.

Well then we all got to talking about how none of us knew our neighbors, and how little time we had—work, go out to dinner, and watch a little TV—and then add in the commute time, shopping, and leaving a little space for private quiet time, well that just about ate up our day. Come to think about it, it just about ate up our week, our month, and our years.

So the next thing you know, somebody says, "why can't we combine all this? Why can't we get white neighbors together, and then get black neighbors together, and then get groups of white neighbors to visit groups of black neighbors. That way, we can get existing neighbors to meet one another for a purpose—to discuss a possible social encounter across racial lines." Well, then, as you might expect the chorus of naysayers just about drowned that idea. The main objection seemed to be that nobody would buy it. "It would be like throwing a party and nobody came."

Now the thing you have to remember is this. I'm talking about the 1990s. The former Soviet Union had collapsed, and our country was on an economic roll—unemployment was way down, as were interest rates, and things looked pretty good to a lot of business people. As I mentioned earlier, there were plenty of problems, including race relations. But in some respects, we were pretty much in agreement that if anybody was going to try to improve race relations in America, the turn of the century was a good time to try.

I won't bore you with all the details, but we finally decided to take the idea to a few prominent downtown boosters. A couple of them liked the idea and agreed to raise the funds to staff the program. One of them suggested that we were thinking too small, that we shouldn't limit ourselves just to neighborhoods, but that we should line up businesses, churches, non-profits, any group we could think of. We figured if we could involve 20,000 people per year over 10 years, we could substantially change the climate in the inner city.

The first year out we met our goal. People were meeting in homes, churches, clubs, an armory, school classrooms. We set up schedules, provided maps, and provided biographical sketches of the participants.

The second year out was even more amazing. Thirty-five thousand people participated. We had to use school buses on some evenings just to move some of the people around. Participation began to drop off after that, so that in year five, when only 5,000 people participated, we shut the program down. All told, less than 100,000 people participated. But that was okay. We accomplished what we wanted to do.

The first thing we noticed—I mean within a couple of months out of the gate—we started getting more inquiries from companies indicating they were considering relocating to our town. Almost at the same time, we noticed increased turnover in downtown land ownership. In retrospect, it is easy to see that business people started to get excited about downtown investment opportunities just as soon as they were convinced we were serious about confronting the racial divide. Well you don't need me to tell you what happened after that. Just look around outside. The condos, apartments, offices, theaters, restaurants, art galleries, hotels—much of this was built in the last 12 years.

Some other things happened too, but they weren't as easy to spot. I'm not really sure how to say this—people just sort of started treating one another better. And also just generally acting more responsibly.

The evidence was everywhere. Crime was down, education was up. There were fewer unwed mothers. Birthrates declined, but immigration was up. Wife and child battering were down, drugs were down, abortions were down. Growth in prison population and gated communities continued, but the rate of growth declined. The homeless and mental health issues continued to befuddle us, but the big picture looked pretty good.

Actually, it was better than pretty good. People in our town just seemed to get along better, be more respectful of one another. Many said that was because we were putting more criminals in jail for more years, had eliminated welfare as a way of life, and in other ways had forced people to be more responsible for their own lives.

I don't doubt that each of these aspects played a part. But I'm convinced that the most important factor that brought this community together was the city-wide dialogue. A number of us had been around for years, and we just had the feeling that the time was ripe. I mean we just felt that a lot of people wanted to improve our relationships with black people, but just didn't know how to get started. We had always had corporate leaders who were "committed to downtown" and supportive of "affirmative action" and "helping the less fortunate." But that had always been a mixed bag. The CEOs' primary responsibilities were to shareholders—they were playing with other people's money—which placed real limits on what they could do consistent with their roles as fiduciaries. Mandatory affirmative action was as much defensive as offensive. CEOs needed the cover of law to make sure their own "affirmative action" didn't place them at a competitive disadvantage to other firms who were less high-minded.

And, much as I hate to say it, "helping the less fortunate" had always been a mixed bag too. We Yankees had always called it the plantation mentality—sort of "noblesse oblige"—the obligation of the "haves" to take care of the "have nots." That was a basic rationale offered by plantation owners in maintaining support for black slavery in the nineteenth century. The problem with that approach was that it permanently branded black Americans as presumptively incompetent. But we Yankees were no better in that regard than the southerners, and we applied it across the board. The worst examples took place in the public schools. Basically, after the courts ordered school integration, we dumbed down the curriculum. Since we "knew" that blacks were incompetent, we simply lowered the standards for blacks. Then, in order to be fair, we lowered the standards for everyone else. Then, in order to be fair, we made everything else equal too—everybody's language, culture, and history was equal to everybody else's. We called it multiculturalism. There were no standards—no absolutes—pre-marital sex, guns, violence—no rules. We almost quit on the public school system.

Of course, I have absolutely no way of proving what I am about to say. But I'm going to say it anyway. You can get away with saying things a lot more easily when you're retiring and moving on in years.

I think the community dialogue did more to help our town than anything else we did the last ten years or so. I would like to take some credit for this, but I can't really. The dialogues were started just to get people comfortable with one another and comfortable about coming downtown. But what actually happened was really amazing. White people started entering black people's homes. Why the laughter? Oh, of course, I misspoke myself. White people were invited into the homes of black people, and vice versa. White people were invited to black neighborhoods, and vice versa. From that point on, the dialogues almost didn't matter. A peer relationship had been established – man-to-man, family-to-family. It turned out to be the most respectful thing we ever could have done.

Now here's the part I can't prove, but I firmly believe it. Black fathers became elevated in their own homes and in their own communities. Black children began to look upon their parents with a whole new level of admiration. Black family values, which had traditionally been strong and conservative, began to reassert themselves. When black fathers insisted that homework be completed, they spoke from the additional strength provided by white community validation. It's perverse, really, when you think about it. We had created an environment that had placed undue pressure on the black community. Once the pressure was relieved, things got better rapidly.

The most obvious reaction in the black community involved the public schools. I say "reaction" because although there had been for some time a call from the black community for higher educational standards and literacy, the call became a clamor. Teacher competency and student performance became paramount concerns. In turn, white community leaders became reenergized about the prospects for public education and, if I might say so, American ideals and exceptionalism too.

Now mind you, all this took place over a period of years. And most of us in the business community were just giddy about our good fortune for which we could take no credit. You see, there were out in the community a number of myths about business, not the least of which was the concept of the "pie." According to this community myth, there was only one economic pie in each community, and it always remained the same size. The idea was that the only way to get a bigger slice of the pie was to either take it from someone else, or have it given to you by someone else. Many people made a living telling this story.

Now we business people knew this was a myth: we knew that pies could not only get bigger, but they could multiply. Well, you know, you can't fight myths, so we didn't try to. But we weren't surprised when our community really took off economically. Of course we never were able to figure out whether business brought people in or people brought business in; probably some of both. You may not remember this, but we used to do a lot of convention business in our town. Things finally got so good here that we reduced our reliance on the convention business. Oh, we still had plenty of tourists, all right, but they came as families to visit our city, to enjoy our parks and the other things we had built. We didn't entirely get out of the convention business, you understand, but we became a lot more selective about who we went after. Some of our convention space was converted to urban schools and indoor playgrounds.

Oh my gosh! I have just rambled on and on! I am so sorry. Please forgive me. I've overstayed my welcome. Thank you so much for staying to hear me out. And thank you so much for my award. God bless you all.

NINETEEN

Almost all of what you have read so far was drafted prior to the year 2000. By early 1999, I had decided to submit the manuscript draft to a publisher for review. The publisher responded with the following rejection letter:

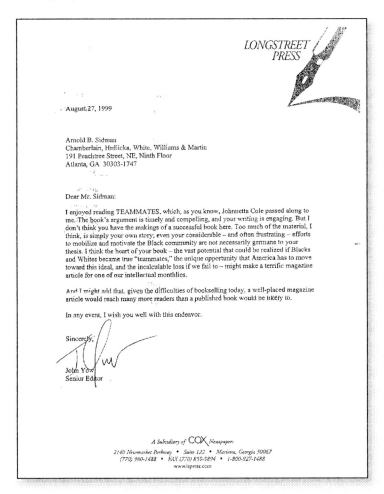

LONGSTREET PRESS

August 27, 1999

Arnold B. Sidman
Chamberlain, Hrdlicka, White, Williams & Martin
191 Peachtree Street, NE, Ninth Floor
Atlanta, GA 30303-1747

Dear Mr. Sidman:

I enjoyed reading TEAMMATES, which, as you know, Johnnetta Cole passed along to me. The book's argument is timely and compelling, and your writing is engaging. But I don't think you have the makings of a successful book here. Too much of the material, I think, is simply your own story; even your considerable – and often frustrating – efforts to mobilize and motivate the Black community are not necessarily germane to your thesis. I think the heart of your book – the vast potential that could be realized if Blacks and Whites became true "teammates," the unique opportunity that America has to move toward this ideal, and the incalculable loss if we fail to – might make a terrific magazine article for one of our intellectual monthlies.

And I might add that, given the difficulties of bookselling today, a well-placed magazine article would reach many more readers than a published book would be likely to.

In any event, I wish you well with this endeavor.

Sincerely,

John Yow
Senior Editor

A Subsidiary of COX Newspapers
2140 Newmarket Parkway • Suite 122 • Marietta, Georgia 30067
(770) 980-1488 • FAX (770) 859-9894 • 1-800-927-1488
www.lspress.com

I considered the publisher's critique quite fair. More to the point, the rejection caused me to rethink the project. I was not primarily interested in becoming a published author. What I wanted to do was to turn some variation of the "Joe Civic" story into a reality. I therefore temporarily abandoned the publication project and embarked on a crusade to do just that.

In his letter, John Yow had suggested preparing an article suitable for publication in an "intellectual" monthly. With that suggestion in mind, I drafted just such a piece for pitching one-on-one to individuals I would endeavor to enlist in the crusade. After numerous conversations, the revised proposal was reduced to this:

It is hereby proposed that a community-wide effort be initiated to improve social relations between blacks and whites in Atlanta. Such an effort would be based upon the following self-evident propositions: life is a team game and we are Team America; our team would improve its performance and have more fun playing if we had better social relations between African-Americans and white Americans; and Atlanta is the best place to initiate such an effort.

Georgia Governor-elect Perdue was quoted prior to his inauguration as follows: "The whole state is the team, and I want us to move together as a team."

It is probably fair to say neither most African-Americans nor most white Americans would characterize the relationship between our putative groups as one between teammates. But it might also be fair to say life in America would be significantly enhanced if we could indeed see one another as such.

The teammate paradigm is a useful construct. Most of us have played on teams, and we know that making and keeping a place on a team is a competitive struggle. We know each member of a team is both expected and obligated to contribute to its success, and a team can be expected to carry a failing teammate for just so long. We know team spirit is an important factor in both individual and team performance. And we know being on a winning team is a lot more satisfying and enjoyable than being on a team that is struggling.

But team members do not become teammates merely by virtue of being issued common uniforms and equipment. Teammate status implies trust and respect which must be communicated by deeds, not words.

Allow me to put this proposal in context. It is difficult to imagine a nation more worthy of the appellation "chosen people." Whether by the grace of God, or an accident of history, or some combination thereof, our country has since its inception represented the best chance for mankind to learn how to live together in mutual respect, succor, and peace.

We did not invent the principles by which we live: limited federal representative government by the people; each person enjoying equality before the law. But we were the first major nation to actualize them.

Why did we actualize them? What is it about the American character that impelled us to fight, and to fight again and again, to institute and then to try to preserve these principles?

Tocqueville, perhaps the keenest observer of the young America, provided these possible answers around the year 1830:

[Americans] care about each of their country's interests as if it were their own. Each man takes pride in the nation; the successes it gains seem his own work, and he becomes elated. . . .

He trusts fearlessly in his own powers, which seem to him sufficient for everything. . . . No doubt he is often less successful than the state would have been in his place, but in the long run the sum of all private undertakings far surpasses anything the government might have done. . . .

The common man in the United States has understood the influence of the general prosperity on his own happiness, an idea so simple but nevertheless so little understood by [other] people. . . . To take a hand in the government of society and to talk about it is his most important business and, so to say, the only pleasure he knows . . . .

At the same time, Tocqueville was careful to point out that none of this had anything to do with black Americans:

The Negro makes a thousand fruitless efforts to insinuate himself into a society that repulses him; he adapts himself to his oppressors' tastes, adopting their opinions and hoping by imitation to join their community. From birth he has been told that his race is naturally inferior to the white man and almost believing that, he holds himself in contempt.

One hundred and eighty years later, it appears that black Americans have just about given up trying to "insinuate" themselves into white society, resorting instead to appeals to white conscience, black power, and the federal government.

As presently envisioned, the proposal contemplates enlisting the organized faith community to provide the venues and formats whereby church, synagogue and mosque members would meet for a wide variety of social get-togethers conducive to conversation. The religious institutions could be recruited and paired or matched to minimize transportation issues and maximize neighborhood affinity. Recruitment, marketing, security, public relations and documentation, and other logistical issues could be addressed and managed by any one or a combination of longstanding civic engagement institutions, such as the Metro Atlanta Chamber of Commerce, Central Atlanta Progress, and Leadership Atlanta. Ideally, tens of thousands of participants would deliver the message that, at least in Atlanta, black and white Americans are teammates.

If this proposal were implemented, I would hope for the following: community leaders would become encouraged to reassert and broaden their message that being an educated, accountable citizen is a worthy goal, and this message would be more broadly embraced; affirmative action mandated by law would be eliminated and replaced by affirmative action voluntarily pursued as a smart business practice; and private support for public education, redevelopment of our central city and our transportation network would be increased. I would also hope to put a major crimp in the politics of racial division and to confound the Yankee hypocrites. And finally, I would hope we might somehow return to that time when Tocqueville observed that what set America apart from the rest of the western world was the self-reliant, public-spirited mien of its people:

> As soon as several Americans have conceived a senti-
> ment or an idea that they want to produce before the
> world, they seek each other out, and when found, they
> unite. Thenceforth they are no longer isolated individu-
> als, but a power conspicuous from the distance whose
> actions serve as an example; when it speaks, men
> listen.[16]

We know, of course, that words and talk are cheap and that the
proposal entails some risks, not the least of which is a public display of lack of interest on the part of either the white or black communities or both. But we also know there are real risks associated
with continuing to drift in matters of race relations. In any event,
I am confident that if Atlanta's community leaders commit to the
task, it will be done.

We know we are not asking too much of our fellow citizens. Almost
all of the heavy lifting has already been performed by our forefathers:
discovery of the land, independence, government formed and constrained by a constitution, a union forged in blood, and defense of our
way of life in wars fought all over the world. And yet, our forefathers
did not complete the task of nation building, and to my mind it is
now time to address the issue of intergroup relations between blacks
and whites. Our black fellow-citizens have never had the home field
advantage. No unilateral action on their part can attain it. We owe it
to ourselves and our posterity to deny it to them no longer.

Over a two-year period, I had lunch or in-office conversations
with many individuals, both black and white, in search of visible
support for the proposal. Each of these people was either a recognized community leader or only one degree separated from such.
As a group, they were almost unanimous in either denying the

efficacy of or need for the proposal, or stressing its low probability of success: "too simplistic," "too contrived," and "too utopian" were the voiced objections. The few who thought the idea was at least worthy of pursuit were unanimous in their unwillingness to personally participate in the effort: "I gave up after dealing with public housing"; "I'm from out of town and not the right sect"; and "this is not just an uphill battle you're talking about—this is a sheer cliff" are phrases that exemplify the gap between where I was and where they were.

Most of the people I spoke to had been alive during the civil rights era, and I felt they could better appreciate both how far we had come and how much farther we had to go in the matter of race relations. I had also hoped that my generation of white men would feel the greatest obligation to improve race relations as a part of "giving back" to the community. However, as my frustration mounted in the face of the unremitting negativity, I began to broaden my search for support to any person I thought might help. Over the years, none of these forays panned out, although one encounter portrayed the toll visited on my psyche by not only the unyielding resistance to the proposal, but also the seeming indifference to seeing the issue as very important in the grand scheme of things. The encounter involved my conversation with a *bona fide* community leader-in-training who was well-respected within the Atlanta business community. I had every reason to believe he would be intrigued by the proposal when he indicated his willingness not only to consider it, but to read my draft manuscript. When we met again following his review of the draft, I was encouraged by his conclusion that my efforts appeared admirable to him. But it was his boss—an acknowledged business leader in the community—whose involvement in the project I needed. So I asked, "What about your boss? Do you think he would be willing to get involved in this project?" With only a moment's reflection, he responded, "No, I don't think so."

It was at that moment that I lost it. I responded with this subdued diatribe: "I understand. Your boss would probably be concerned that his involvement might injure his reputation. That's where I have an advantage—being Jewish, I don't have a reputation to lose!" My interlocutor was speechless, of course, and I was immediately remorseful for using such uncalled for invective. But the damage was done. I stood revealed as, at best, an ingrate, and my confidant had been punished for his good deed. I was too embarrassed to apologize, and, in any event, as my mother said, "sorry doesn't help."

Over the next few years, I had far fewer conversations about race, but my obsession persisted. And, over time, I was able to put together a small but highly qualified core of black and white citizen leaders and their spouses who were at least willing to discuss the possibility of initiating some kind of positive community effort aimed at promoting improved race relations.

The most visible participant and his wife kindly offered to host dinner at their home near downtown Atlanta. He also offered to augment our number by bringing to the table a highly visible local politician, presumably to add some stature to the group. At this stage of my life, my experience and cynicism had combined to make me wary of all politicians regardless of political party. Nevertheless, in deference to our host, I agreed to brief the politico. Now armed with a one-page version of the proposal, the three of us met over lunch. The politician said she liked the teammates concept.

The dinner was delightful. The food and conversation were delightful. Then we got to the nitty-gritty. Each attendee was given a chance to speak about how to proceed. There was no common denominator; no dialogue, just a series of disjointed monologues. I did not speak—my proposal was ostensibly the reason for the get-together, but you would never have guessed that from the disparate views offered. Finally, the politician spoke. Turning her head to face me directly, her first words were, "I don't know you." I assume the unspoken part of her thought was ". . . therefore, why should I trust you?" I was both humiliated and vindicated simultaneously.

The dinner ended shortly thereafter. No one suggested we reconvene.

TWENTY

Following the tragedy of September 11, 2001, advancing my quixotic quest for improved social relations between blacks and whites in America took a back seat to the more immediate issues of security and asymmetric warfare facing our country. Nevertheless, I continued to maintain a heightened interest in issues related to race. Predictably, I found the issues best framed by conservative commentators such as Thomas Sowell, Shelby Steele and Walter E. Williams. But the palpable lack of progress on racial issues undermined my determination to persevere; the continuing lack of progress in black community achievement in education and other indicia of success was particularly disheartening. The politics of division and big government seemed to be on the ascendancy.

By this time, I had concluded that two issues appeared to be insurmountable. One was that most white Americans remained uncomfortable in social relations with blacks; the second was the black community had by and large accepted racism as the universal explanation for black underachievement.

Of these two issues, I also had concluded that the most important of these to address initially was black underachievement. This was a problem primarily within the control of the black community, and one that could arguably draw psychological strength from black successes in sports and entertainment, and financial support from American businesses and philanthropies. I was convinced the mere creation of visible local black institutions formed to pursue this agenda would energize that portion of the white community committed to black success as fundamental to American success.

Sad to say, these hopes were once again dashed, this time by the treatment accorded Bill Cosby by the black professional community when, in May 2004, he publicly criticized the post-civil rights "accomplishments" of the black heirs of that movement. It appeared that Mr. Cosby was being rebuked not so much for what he said, but because of how he said it and where he said it—publicly. Although ostensibly aimed at lower-class blacks, his critique could easily have been understood as an indictment of black community leadership.

I was particularly demoralized by what I perceived to be a lack of public support for Bill Cosby from within the general black community. I, along with millions of others, had come to appreciate his universal appeal as a comic genius capable of explaining human nature to human beings. As a young father, I had been grateful to him when he shared with me (and many other young fathers) that his young teenage son also had a two-word rejoinder for all criticism directed toward that son— "no problem." At the time, I was comforted by the fact I was not alone in trying to discharge my responsibility to encourage my youngest son to raise his sights. Tragically, I also recalled that Mr. Cosby had lost that son in a seemingly senseless murder on an American highway—arguably just another victim of our societal dysfunction. Even an outsider like me could plainly see that Bill Cosby was a proud and gifted black man with no discernible self-identity psychosis; a charitable man supportive of his people; and an exemplar of an eminently successful black professional having the courage to challenge the myriad vested interests associated with the continuation of black victimhood.

In any event, the Bill Cosby episode, coupled with my protracted failures which preceded that episode, convinced me that it was time to bid my racial harmony obsession good-bye.

●　●　●

That's the problem with obsessions. I thought I could dismiss the obsession. I was wrong: the obsession controls the person's mind, not the other way around.

It wasn't the election of President Barack Obama that made me realize my obsession was still in control of me. I was not surprised by his election. Professional politicians are primarily entertainers, and Senator Obama was far and away the most intelligent, charismatic, personable, plainspoken presidential candidate running for office in 2008. But his election certainly did not represent any broad referendum on black and white relations in America. White Americans had been voting by virtual secret ballot in favor of black entertainers for many decades.

But, indirectly, it was President Obama who reignited my commitment to publish this book. More to the point, on Wednesday, February 18, 2009, in Remarks as Prepared for Delivery by Attorney General Eric Holder at the Department of Justice African American History Month Program, the following statements were made:

> Though this nation has proudly thought of itself as an ethnic melting pot, in things racial we have always been and continue to be, in too many ways, essentially a nation of cowards. Though race related issues continue to occupy a significant portion of our political discussion, and though there remain many unresolved racial issues in this nation, we, average Americans, simply do not talk enough with each other about race. It is an issue we have never been at ease with and given our nation's history this is in some ways understandable. And yet, if we are to make progress in this area we must feel comfortable enough with one another, and tolerant enough of each other, to have frank conversations about the racial matters that continue to divide us. . . .
>
> As a nation we have done a pretty good job in melding the races in the workplace. We work with one another, lunch together and, when the event is at the workplace during work hours or shortly thereafter, we socialize with one another

fairly well, irrespective of race. And yet even this interaction operates within certain limitations. We know, by "American instinct" and by learned behavior, that certain subjects are off limits and that to explore them risks, at best embarrassment, and, at worst, the questioning of one's character. And outside the workplace the situation is even more bleak in that there is almost no significant interaction between us.

Based on my more than 20 years' experience having private conversations about race, it is obvious to me that neither black nor white community leaders feel that conversations between blacks and whites *about race* will produce anything worth the risk of engaging in such conversations. On the other hand, I am encouraged by evidence that some of my black teammates have acknowledged the utter failure of various post-civil rights programs and institutions, and encouraged blacks to engage in some introspection followed by private action. I refer specifically to Debra Dickerson's *The End of Blackness* (Pantheon Books, 2004; Anchor Books, 2005), Stuart Buck's *Acting White* (Yale University Press, 2009), and Tom Burrell's *Brainwashed* (Smiley Books, 2010). These and other similar efforts are worthy of our appreciation and support. Maybe Bill Cosby was onto something.

EPILOGUE

When I entered corporate America in 1968, fresh from my four-year apprenticeship with the IRS Chief Counsel's office, I was introduced to a number of business-related clichés, *i.e.*, once effective ideas spoiled from long familiarity or so worn out by overuse as to become dull or meaningless. My favorite was this: "50 percent of the money we spend on advertising is useless and wasteful—we just don't know which 50 percent this is."

This cliché also applies to government expenditures, particularly those made by the U.S. federal government. During the 1950s, the story was told of a U.S. Interior Department employee hosting a visitor from the Midwest who wanted to see the government at work. During a tour of the Interior Department, everyone seemed to be doing something except one employee, who was crying his eyes out. The visitor asked his host if he could explain this aberrant behavior. "Yes, I can," said the host. "His Indian died. He's out of a job."

In 1997, the U.S. Office of Management and Budget issued a paper describing the status of President Clinton's National Performance Review of the federal government.[17] This review, initiated in 1993, was led by Vice President Al Gore under the auspices of an interagency task force. The paper was forthright in describing the inherent flaw in the study: the task force "agreed to narrow our focus to 'how' government works and avoid 'what' government should be doing." Even constrained by this misguided focus ("the vision was to 'create a government that works better and costs less' based on the four principles of putting customers first, cutting red tape, empowering employees, and cutting back to basics"), the task force proposed "to cut overhead positions in the government in half." Part of the impetus for these suggestions may have come from the task force's acknowledgment that "in 1963, more than 75 percent of the public thought the federal government did the right thing most of the time. By 1993, it was less than 20 percent."

Regardless of whether we believe the government has most of the answers, some of the answers, or almost none of the answers to our problems, we must acknowledge that government at all levels is absolutely out of control and unmanageable. A 2003 study of the federal government workforce concluded there were almost 17 million people performing federal government work.[18] These included civilian and military personnel, contractors, grant recipients, state and local workers, and postal employees. Numerous studies by Congress, academics and other non-governmental organizations have identified overwhelming evidence of abuse of government programs by both providers and recipients of federal benefits. Fraud and corruption are inherent in such programs, regardless of whether the providers or recipients are individuals or businesses. There is a complete lack of accountability for performance by government because there are no valid measures of performance. And even if there were such measures, why would any professional politician want to use them? Why would any politico want to voluntarily relinquish the power that comes with the ability to direct billions of dollars of other people's money?

This is not to say, of course, that the private sector is immune to these malefactions, abuses, and irresistible impulses. But there are two critical distinctions between government and non-government activity. First, government has the power to tax and regulate, which citizens cannot easily avoid. Second, government activity and effectiveness is almost impossible to measure, control, or even understand. The political theater and shenanigans that feed our escapism are just that. Government, because of its colossal size and complexity, operates essentially by exception, lurching from one public failure to the next. On the other hand, the private sector is primarily based upon mutual consent and has some measure of accountability through the profit and loss system—which more or less works until the government decides the private sector actor is either too big, or too politically connected, to fail.

What has all of this to do with teammates and blacks and whites in America? Our country was founded by people who valued freedom over security. Over time, and perhaps accelerating following the Great Depression of the 1930s, we came more and more to value security over freedom. And politicians were more than delighted to oblige. Over time, the concept of security was broadened by us to include just about anything we didn't want to do or think about. And politicians were more than delighted to oblige. They forced children into integrated schools before their parents were prepared to do so, and scapegoated southerners in the process. They enacted and enforced affirmative action laws, and broadened them to include all minorities and women as political cover. And they expanded government employment in part to provide a dignified form of welfare. All of this because we chose to abdicate our responsibility as citizens.

And what have we to show for this? Undoubtedly, some black men have achieved business or employment success beyond what they might have achieved in the absence of affirmative action mandated by law. But what we have thus far lost is the opportunity to voluntarily assimilate black Americans into mainstream America. The idea that we could do so in sports and entertainment but not in other important areas of our lives is patently absurd. In the meantime, power-hungry, self-absorbed politicians have engaged in various forms of self-aggrandizement by convincing first themselves and then us, their inferiors, that they have the answers. We know, of course, they do not have the answers, but it is so much easier to just let them deal with the mess.

Given my unblemished record of failure concerning the matter of blacks and whites in America, I should be at least somewhat reticent to make any further suggestions in this regard. But, like government at all levels, I am out of control.

Fundamentally, my views on this subject have not changed over the past 30 years. I still believe the black community needs to rethink its priorities. Racism will never be eliminated, but it has abated. Given our history of slavery, discrimination, and segregation, white and black discomfort in a social setting is more than understandable. Also understandable is the black desire for equality of results masked by the euphemism of equal opportunity. But continued reliance upon victimization and white guilt as a primary strategy for survival is no longer, if it ever was, a winning strategy.

Nowhere do the abdication of white responsibility, the congenital failures of government, and the need for employment opportunities for our black teammates coalesce in a more hideous form than in the public schools. At some point in time, the public schools began to shift focus from being primarily educators of children to being primarily employers of adults. And most of these employees are either members of a labor union, or an employee association similar to a union, or have jobs covered by contracts with such organizations. These organizations, which include the National Education Association and the American Federation of Teachers, have enormous political clout, as do other labor unions representing primarily government employees. Labor unions, which represent approximately 40 percent of government workers but less than 10 percent of private sector employees, are primarily about jobs, not performance.[19]

By any meaningful measure, public schools are producing unsatisfactory results for students, particularly for black students in urban centers. In a different world, my white teammates would not have allowed our public schools to deteriorate in this fashion. But in this world, my white teammates simply created a parallel private school universe and invited a selected number of my black teammates to join. Problem solved?

I am convinced a primary cause of our public school debacle and the cancer-like growth of government is white flight and denial and black despair. I do agree with Eric Holder that my white and black teammates should converse with one another. But first, I would suggest my white teammates and my black teammates each talk separately amongst themselves.

It really doesn't matter what I think. My white teammates will need to privately decide whether black employment and public school performance merit our attention, or whether it might help our performance as a nation if social relations between blacks and whites in America simply improved. If we decide to address these issues, we might consider the fact that, as of September 30, 2009, black employees represented 17.8 percent of the federal workforce, but only 9.8 percent of the civilian labor force.[20] By the same token, my black teammates will need to privately decide whether they need a new game plan. If they decide to address this issue, it might help my white teammates decide whether we wish to address our issues. It is a dialectical process.

In any event, if we decide to continue down the path to nowhere, I hope we will at least have the decency to cease travelling around the world trying to teach other people how to live.

ENDNOTES

Chapter 2

1.*Atlanta Journal-Constitution,* July 4, 1997, G-5

Chapter 3

2. *See generally Barry Schwartz,* George Washington: The Making of An American Symbol *(Cornell University Press, 1987)*

3. Current, Williams, Freidel, Brinkley, *A Survey: American History* (6th Ed.) (Alfred A. Knopf, New York, 1983) 375, quoting John L. O'Sullivan (1845)

Chapter 5

4. The Report of the National Advisory Commission on Civil Disorders, or "Kerner Report" (1968); Report Summary, Part I, Ch. 2 (New York: Bantam Books, 1968)

Chapter 7

5. Abba Eban, *My People: The Story of the Jews* (Random House, 1984), 503-04

6. "Israel: A Nation Under Siege," *Time Magazine,* June 9, 1967; "Middle East: The Quickest War, *Time Magazine,* June 16, 1967

Chapter 8

7. Carter B. Cue, archivist, "Clarence Gaines: A Brief Historical Sketch of a Legend," Winston-Salem State University Archives (Feb. 2, 1998)

Chapter 9

8. Burrough & Helyar, *Barbarians At The Gate* (Harper & Row, 1990), 83

9. *Orlando Sentinel,* July 9, 1990, A-5

Chapter 10

10. *Plessy v. Ferguson* (1896), 163 U.S. 537

11. Gunnar Myrdal, *An American Dilemma* (Harper & Row, 1994; Twentieth Anniversary Edition, 1962), 167-68, 1021

Chapter 11

12. Theodore Cross, *The Black Power Imperative* (Faulkner Books, 1987)

Chapter 16

13. Myrdal, *An American Dilemma,* 29, 97-98

14. Thernstrom and Thernstrom, *America In Black and White* (Simon & Schuster, 1997), 530

Chapter 17

15. Eric Siblin, "Unity Plea 'Bogus,' " *Winnipeg Free Press*, October 27, 1995, 17

Chapter 19

16. Alexis de Tocqueville, *Democracy In America* (Harper & Row, 1966, ed. J. P. Mayer), 95, 237, 243, 319, 516

Epilogue

17. John Kamensky, *The U.S. Reform Experience: The National Performance Review,* presentation notes, Indiana University, April 6, 1997

18. Paul C. Light, "Fact Sheet on the New True Size of Government," Sept. 5, 2003; cited in Chris Edwards, "Downsizing the Federal Government," *Policy Analysis* No. 515, June 2, 2004 (Cato Institute)

19. Hirsch and Macpherson, Directory of U.S. Labor Organizations (App. A: BLS Union Membership and Earnings Data, Table 3, 196 (2010))

20. *Fiscal Year 2009 Federal Equal Opportunity Recruitment Program Report to the Congress*, U.S. Office of Personnel Management, 11